Aliens

Encounters with the Unexplained

Aliens

Encounters with the Unexplained

Marcus Day

CLB

CREDITS

AT QUADRILLION PUBLISHING LTD:

Commissioning Editors:
Will Steeds and Philip de Ste Croix
Project Editor:
Suzanne Evins
Production:
Neil Randles, Ruth Arthur

AT PARAGON PUBLISHING LTD:

Project Co-ordinator:
Richard Monteiro
Art Director:
Mark Kendrick
Project Editor:
Geoff Harris
Picture Research:
Marcus Day

5012 Aliens: Encounters with the Unexplained
This edition published in 1998 by CLB
© 1997 CLB International

Printed and bound in Italy
ISBN 1-85833-662-7

INTRODUCTION

THE PHENOMENAL SUCCESS OF TV PROGRAMS AND MOVIES such as *The X Files* and *Independence Day* is proof that interest in extraterrestrial life is at a height unequaled since the flying saucer scares of the 1950s. As the new millennium approaches, the paranormal has become one of the most fiercely debated subjects in the developed world, especially as the number of reports of UFO sightings and alien abductions is steadily mounting. To help the newcomer to Ufology make sense of the mass of evidence for and against UFOs, *Aliens: Encounters with the Unexplained* is a comprehensive introduction to this highly complex and controversial subject.

Rather than overload readers with the sheer weight of anomalous phenomena that have been recorded over the years, the book is divided into six chapters, dealing with the most renowned Close Encounters of the First Kind through to the Fifth, and finishing off with a chapter dedicated to UFO hot spots – those otherwise unrelated parts of the world that seem to attract more than their fair share of UFO sightings. Should you ever see a UFO or would simply like to explore the subject further, there's also a full list of investigative groups worldwide.

This book covers a huge range of episodes, dealing with sightings from the dawn of time right up to the most astonishing sightings of 1996. All the most (in)famous cases are included, from the Belgian Triangle to the Siberian Fireball, as well as a lot of new material that has never been published before. This is coupled with some truly breathtaking photographs of UFO phenomena, gathered from every continent.

Much has been written on the subject of UFOs since Kenneth Arnold's sighting of a UFO flotilla in 1947, but the believers and the skeptics seem as far apart as ever. The purpose of *Aliens: Encounters with the Unexplained* is to show that, while no-one can provide absolute proof that alien races are visiting our planet, the weight of evidence suggesting some kind of deliberate contact is overwhelming. This book will also illustrate how seriously the world's governments have been taking the possibility of extraterrestrial visitors, sometimes to the extent of suppressing eye-witness reports or spreading dis-information. The motives behind such deceit are unclear: maybe the authorities fear concrete evidence of UFO contact would spark mass panic, or perhaps some sinister conspiracy is taking place.

Whatever the truth, *Aliens: Encounters with the Unexplained* presents some of the strongest proof yet that we are not alone in the universe. And as many of the cases suggest, perhaps it's time to stop arguing about alien visitors and start listening to them: one of the strongest themes in the messages given to those people who've interacted with extraterrestrials is that mankind has to start taking better care of the planet or some major catastrophe threatens to engulf us all. At the very least, after reading *Aliens: Encounters with the Unexplained*, I guarantee you'll look up at the night sky with a new interest.

Marcus Day

CONTENTS

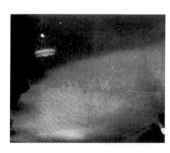

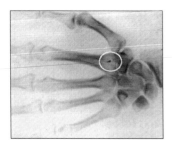

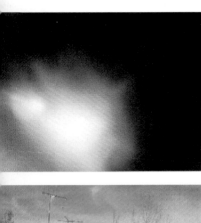

CHAPTER ONE

CLOSE ENCOUNTERS OF THE FIRST KIND

ACCORDING TO THE INFLUENTIAL UFOLOGIST DR J. ALLEN Hynek, there are five categories for classifying encounters with UFOs or aliens. Close Encounters of the First Kind refer to a UFO spotted within 150 yards. Close Encounters of the Second Kind are those in which a UFO leaves behind evidence of its presence, such as scorch marks on the ground or fragments of alien material. Close Encounters of the Third Kind are those in which a UFO is spotted with visible occupants. Close Encounters of the Fourth Kind involve abduction by aliens, and Close Encounters of the Fifth Kind involve direct communication between humans and aliens.

This first chapter will deal with UFO sightings which at first glance appear to be nothing more than lights in the sky. Some of the classic cases include the Star of Bethlehem – was this a star or a UFO under intelligent guidance? Then there are the Lubbock Lights, which have gone down in history as possibly the most baffling appearance of anomalous lights ever recorded on film. Hundreds of eye-witnesses reported bizarre light formations over Lubbock, Texas, in the 1950s and numerous photos were taken, many of which have been proven not to be fakes.

Almost everyone interested in UFOs will know of the enigmatic Area 51 and the many anomalous lights that have been spotted around this mysterious "air force base" – just what's going on deep in the Nevada desert? According to Bob Lazar, who claims to be an ex-employee of the top-secret facility, crashed UFOs are held there and carefully "back engineered" so similar technology can be used in the latest military aircraft. Lazar says he made his amazing claims public in a desperate attempt to discourage any assassination attempts from the US government, who were furious that he had revealed what he knew about Area 51. Outside the US, some startling photographs of UFOs have emerged from Russia, and are now public knowledge following the collapse of the Soviet Union. The tiny village of Moljebka really is a phenomenon in its own right – balls of light are frequently seen in the vicinity and there are even claims that UFOs have landed and that aliens have been photographed.

Of course, there are several possible natural explanations for odd lights in the sky, such as atmospheric phenomena. Lenticular and noctiluscent clouds, for example, can look remarkably like UFOs.

FIRE IN THE SKY

ALTHOUGH NOT IN the strictest sense a Close Encounter of the First Kind, the case of the "Siberian Fireball" does exhibit many traits which could label it a "CE1." The only witnesses to this remarkable event described a glowing blue fireball, the only sounds audible were similar to a sonic explosion. Granted, the event was followed by widespread devastation, which, if the fireball was a UFO, would categorize the event as a Close Encounter of the Third Kind.

Around 7 am on 30th June 1908, the passengers of the Trans-Siberian Express were amazed to witness what came to be known as the Great Siberian Fireball. The train carriages shook violently as the bright blue fireball roared overhead, while the driver thought that the loud noises and vibrating coming from the rear of his carriage were actually the sounds of his train exploding. Yet the occupants of the Trans-Siberian Express were not the only ones to witness the largest known fireball in recorded history.

By 7:15 am the fireball had reached the isolated Siberian trading post of Vanavara. S. B. Semenow, a local farmer, was sitting on his porch enjoying the rising midsummer sun whilst his neighbor, P. P. Kosalopov, was doing some exterior decorating. Semenow was quoted as saying that a fireball, which "covered an enormous part of the sky," appeared from a north-westerly direction. Both men fell to the ground, immobilized by pain, as the object passed overhead. Semenow felt that the shirt on his back was on fire while Kosalopov clasped his ears in a vain attempt to quell the burning sensation from within. The fireball was also witnessed by a nomadic Mongolian tribe called the Tungus, who populated the area surrounding the Siberian Tunguska river. As they glanced upwards into the sky they watched as the vast fireball streaked through the atmosphere, leaving a 500-mile trail of smoke and light.

SOUNDS LIKE THUNDER

Within seconds, the fireball finally came to rest in a desolate region of bogs and pine-covered hills traversed by the Tunguska river, 60 miles north of Vanavara. Semenow and Kosalopov covered their eyes as the object shattered in a series of blinding flashes, swiftly followed by a "pillar of fire" which reached so high that it could be seen hundreds of miles away.

The sheer force of the explosion produced devastating ground tremors which knocked Semenow off his porch and rained great chunks of earth upon Kosalopov's house. Both men took a few minutes to gather their wits as sounds like thunder rumbled ominously in the air. Around 370 miles to the south, in Kansk, reports told of horses being thrown to the ground, houses shaking and fishermen being swept from their boats.

The driver of the Trans-Siberian Express was just recovering from his first distressing experience when he was again thrown into turmoil as the ground heaved beneath the tracks. He quickly brought the train to a halt, fearing derailment.

- A spectacularly exploding comet or a stray UFO? Almost 90 years after the "Siberian Fireball" crashed into a remote part of this province, debate still rages. According to Professor Alexander Kazantsev, the fireball was a Martian rocket ship. Kazantsev cited eye-witnesses who claimed a UFO changed course several times before exploding.

- The Tungus tribe were hit the hardest by the fireball's explosion. The tribespeople had to contend with the forest fires that burned for weeks, destroying 625 square miles. They lost entire herds of reindeer and the scorched remains of their tents were scattered across the valley. It was nothing short of miraculous that no-one was actually killed.

ATMOSPHERIC DISTURBANCES

The aftermath of this strange visit didn't only affect the Siberian wilderness. After the fireball's explosion, unusually colorful sunsets and sunrises were reported by many countries in Scandinavia and Western Europe, while the Near East also recorded some eerie night-time effects. Nights of up to 100 times brighter than normal were recorded, as well as crimson hues in the sky. These phenomenal lightshows continued until the night of June 30th, but faint traces could still be seen over an extended period of several weeks. On 1st July a woman from Huntingdon, England, wrote to *The Times* in

BOTH MEN FELL TO THE GROUND, IMMOBILIZED BY PAIN, AS THE OBJECT PASSED OVERHEAD

London, saying that shortly after midnight, "it was possible to read large print indoors .... at about 1:30 am the room was quite light, as if it had been day. It would be interesting if anyone would explain the cause of so unusual a sight." Because the identity of the fireball did not become widely known for many years, the cause of these freak conditions could not be easily explained at the time.

- Russian scientist and mineralogist Leonid Kulik, the founder of meteorite science in Russia, was convinced that the Tunguska fireball was in fact an errant iron meteorite even larger than the one which formed the famous Barringer crater in Arizona around 25,000 years ago. Despite using magnetic probes and drilling for many years, Kulik failed to detect a single ounce of metal either in the area, and it became clear that the mysterious object had never even reached the ground.

FLORENSKY'S FUSION THEORY

After 1945, further research into the Siberian Fireball was continued, this time by the Committee on Meteorites of the Soviet Academy of Sciences. These investigations were headed by Soviet geochemist, Krill Florensky, in 1958, 1961 and 1962.

In 1962, Florensky and his team sifted soil for microscopic particles caused by the burn-up and disintegration of the Tunguska object. This proved to be successful. Florensky discovered a narrow tongue of cosmic dust stretching over 150 miles, north-west of the crash site. The scientists found that thousands of metal particles had been fused together, indicating that the Tunguska fireball had been of a uniform composition. Compositions of this type are believed to be typical of objects such as meteors or shooting stars. On 4 May 1959, Britain's *The Daily Express* published an article about Florensky's expeditions. The article stated that "the theory of a spaceship crashing in the Tunguska area is causing a split among the Soviet Union's leading scientists." Although the article was a thinly veiled attempt to sensationalize the events, it certainly stirred up genuine scientific interest in the area.

Further investigations by Florensky began to cast doubt upon the existence of radiation in the Tunguska area. Accelerations in the growth patterns of the trees and plant life in the area, which had previously been acknowledged as a symptom of radiation, was now considered to be a natural reaction to the intense fires that had raged following the explosion.

Also, the so-called radiation burns suffered by Tungus reindeer herds was similarly dismissed as a by-product of the great flash of heat given out by the blast. Florensky wrote up the results of his expeditions in 1963 in an article entitled 'Did A Comet Collide With The Earth In 1908?' for *Sky & Telescope* magazine. But believers in the nuclear explosion theory point to the investigations carried out by three US physicists in 1965. This team reported an increase in radiocarbon in the tree rings following the Tunguska blast. If the Tunguska blast was indeed of nuclear origin then this excess radiocarbon would be expected.

- Despite Kulik's belief that a meteorite had crashed, the Soviet Academy of Science showed in later scale-model experiments that an aerial explosion was a more likely explanation. A clump of trees, for example, was left standing.

MARS ATTACKS

Despite the lack of hard evidence one way or the other, the theory that the Siberian Fireball was a comet became widely accepted by the scientific community. But this did not stop Professor Aleksandr Kazantsev, with the aid of Professor B. Lapunov, from disguising his own wild theories in a science-fiction book published shortly after the Second World War.

In *A Guest From The Universe*, Kazantsev insisted that the Tunguska fireball was in fact a rocket ship coming from Mars. Part of the evidence that Kazantsev used to justify his claim comprised of various eye-witness reports that claimed the object changed its course a number of times before it exploded. Kazantsev speculated that the aliens had come to collect water from the nearby Lake Baykal, the largest volume of

- The former Soviet regime took UFO reports very seriously, organising nationwide searches for the strange craft that regularly visited this huge nation.

A JAPANESE UFO GROUP CALLED
SAKURA AGREED WITH KAZANTSEV
AND CLAIMED THAT THE TUNGUSKA
FIREBALL WAS THE EXPLOSION OF A
NUCLEAR POWER PLANT
BELONGING TO AN ERRANT SPACE
VEHICLE

• Lake Baykal. Could the UFO that Kazantsev believed caused the Siberian fireball have been heading for the lake to replenish supplies?

fresh water on Earth. He had been accumulating evidence to support his theory for years and even released some details to fellow researchers in Czechoslovakia and Poland.

A Japanese UFO group called SAKURA agreed with Kazantsev and even went so far as to claim that the Tunguska fireball was the explosion of a nuclear power plant belonging to an errant space vehicle. More recently, an aerodynamics expert called Manotskov has lent some strength to the spaceship theory. He stated that the Tunguska fireball was breaking up as it approached the Earth, so that its final speed was almost one mile per second, as opposed to the usual 20 to 40 miles per second for the average meteorite. Kazantsev and Lapunov's theories of a UFO explosion were not taken seriously by the scientific community, even though no totally convincing explanation has ever been broached.

THE GORMAN INCIDENT

One of the most fascinating accounts of an aerial encounter with an unknown light or object came from Lt George F. Gorman of the US air force. The incident took place over Fargo, North Dakota, on 1st October 1948, and lasted for 27 minutes. Gorman had returned from a cross-country flight with his squadron, but had decided to continue flying in order to clock up some extra night-flying time. He was about to land at about 9:00 pm and radioed the control tower for landing instructions. The control tower told him that there was only one other plane in the vicinity, a Piper Cub. Gorman could make out the plane directly below him, but then what he believed to be the tail light of another plane flashed past. Gorman again contacted the control tower, and was again informed that there was no other traffic in the area. He then decided to investigate the mysterious light for himself. He steered his F-51 towards the light, and as soon as he was within 1,000 yards, he noticed the outline of a fuzzy object. The two continued on a collision course until Gorman pulled out and the light flashed above his canopy at about 500 feet. He cut sharply to the right, and again found himself on a collision course with the light. Yet just as it seemed that a collision was inevitable the light shot up vertically and disappeared. The whole incident was confirmed by two air traffic controllers, who noticed the light, and the Piper Cub. They also testified to the light's startling speed.

Gorman stated that the UFO demonstrated "thought" in its maneuvers. Although no rational explanation has ever been put forward for the incident, an investigative team concluded that Gorman was chasing an errant weather balloon. Although why an experienced flyer with hours of night-time experience could ever mistake a fast-moving object for a relatively slow-moving weather balloon remains a baffling mystery.

CE1s Through History

POSSIBLY THE MOST SIGNIFICANT historical event which could be interpreted as a Close Encounter of the First Kind is the Star of Bethlehem, which, the Bible tells us, guided the three wise men to the nativity of Jesus. The star of Bethlehem was clearly no ordinary star: it was not part of the night sky, and simply appeared and disappeared at will.

The first mention of the star appears in Matthew, Chapter 2:1-2:

> NOW WHEN JESUS WAS BORN IN BETHLEHEM OF JUDEA IN THE DAYS OF HEROD THE KING, BEHOLD THERE CAME WISE MEN FROM THE EAST TO JERUSALEM.
> "WHERE IS HE THAT IS BORN KING OF THE JEWS? FOR WE HAVE SEEN HIS STAR IN THE EAST, AND ARE COME TO WORSHIP HIM."

What's strange is that the three wise men had traveled from the east, so how did they see this star in the east – surely from the direction in which they traveled the star would have been sighted in the west. This mistake can probably be put down to poor interpretation of the night sky, rather than any cosmic cover-up. Yet the puzzle deepens when we learn that the three wise men had seen the star suddenly appear, something which is entirely impossible, as stars hold fixed

● Was the Star of Bethlehem celestial fire, as shown in this woodcut, or a UFO?

locations. However, the story becomes even more mysterious when the three wise men describe how the star traveled before them until it was above the location where Jesus was born – at which point the star stopped.

But if the bright light was a star, how did the wise men know above which building it had stopped – such would have been the distance between the star and the stable where Jesus was born that attempting to even pinpoint which city the star was above would have been a major achievement in itself, let alone find the exact location of the newborn. Clearly, the object was not a conventional star, and had to be a lot lower down on the horizon for the wise men to calculate where Jesus was. There is, therefore, a plausible argument that the object which guided the wise men to Jesus was in fact a UFO, under the guidance and control of an intelligent race of aliens. The only other explanation is the traditional Christian one, that it was a miracle from God.

Further evidence that the Star of Bethlehem was no ordinary star emerges when we consider that the three wise men, or magi, would have been astronomers by training, familiar with the night sky. It's very unlikely that all three would mistakenly presume that the object leading their way was a star; it's far more likely that they believed the object to be like a star, so that is what they called it.

THE LUBBOCK LIGHTS

Fast forwarding from biblical times, the most impressive sighting of "nocturnal lights" ever to be recorded and photographed took place in the Texan town of Lubbock during the months of August and September of 1951. Hundreds of eye-witnesses reported bizarre light formations, and some even stated that they could make out the outline of a wing. The first sighting was on 25th August 1951, reported by an employee of the Atomic Energy Commission in Albuquerque, New Mexico. Both the worker and his wife claimed to have seen a huge object with bluish lights on its rear-edge pass overhead. The lights seemed to be as low as 800 feet, and the pair could make out the wing-shape of the object, with bluish-green glowing tail lights. That same evening, several college professors sitting on a porch in Lubbock noticed a semi-circular formation of lights move quickly overhead. After quite a long time the lights suddenly reappeared and were observed to be glowing, bluish in color.

Another Lubbock resident claimed to have seen the same lights on the same evening, clearly making out a large wing-like craft, again with bluish lights on the tail. This sighting is strikingly similar to the earlier sighting in Alberquerque, and was made only minutes after the latter was reported, so the eye-witness couldn't have had any prior knowledge of it.

Over the following two weeks, several people saw the fast moving lights in and around the town. Most of the witnesses agreed that the lights were always about 45° above the northern horizon, traveling through 90°, and disappearing in a few seconds about 45° over the southern horizon. Many observers had no explanation for what they were seeing, including those with an extensive knowledge of the night sky and atmospherics. On the evening of 31st August, a breakthrough was made when amateur photographer Carl Hart Jr managed to capture the lights on film. He took five shots in all, the best being published in the local newspaper. The lights were seemingly flying in formation against the night sky.

The air force conducted a thorough investigation into the lights and the photographs, but never reached a satisfactory conclusion. The shots taken by Carl Hart Jr were examined, as were the negatives, and were found to be untampered with. To date, nobody has been able to offer a rational explanation for the Lubbock Lights.

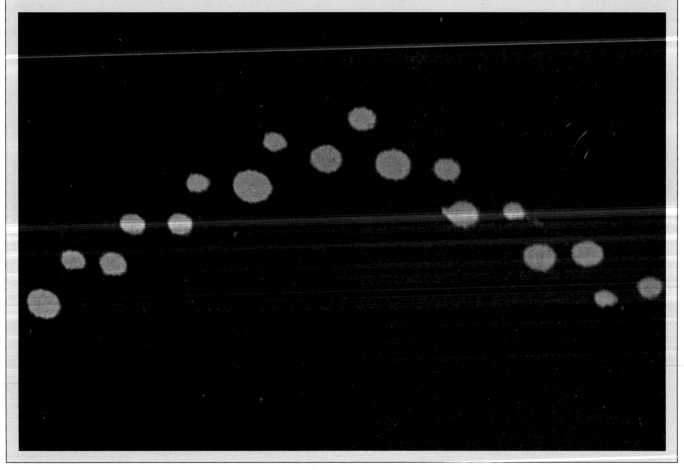

LIFE ON MARS

IT'S OFFICIAL – THERE IS LIFE ON MARS, OR at least there may have been at one time. Scientists have been analyzing meteors that have crashed to Earth, and now believe that the Earth is no longer the only planet in the solar system to have sustained life.

This announcement was made last year by a team of NASA scientists who have recently discovered the fossil of a long-extinct life form. Although this life form was probably only a single-celled organism, it is still proof nonetheless that life did exist on the Red Planet, probably billions of years ago. The organism is believed to have lived in water, trapped below the planet's surface.

NASA launched its latest Mars mission in December 1996, and is hoping the subsequent findings will provide more conclusive proof of basic life.

• Many probes have been launched, yet most of the images proved inconclusive.

The single-celled organism was found in a melon-sized meteorite which was uncovered in 1984 in Antarctica. The composition of the meteorite suggests that it originated in volcanic rock. The dry river beds on the planet suggest that water was present in the past, further evidence that basic life forms were supported. As for the organism, it may have been trapped in the meteorite during a volcanic eruption which would have thrown the rock from the planet's surface. Alternatively, the rock could have been forced into space as the result of a direct meteor strike on Mars. Either of these possibilities would have surely resulted in the organism's death, causing it to fossilize, its outline being preserved in the surrounding rock.

THE MEDIA AND MARS

It would appear that *Discover* magazine, and especially Jack Farmer of the NASA Ames Research Center in California, pre-empted the discovery of life on Mars back in October 1995.

Jack Farmer is the world's only full-time exopaleontologist, a job title he gave to himself, which basically means that he looks for life on other planets. For many years, Farmer has been attending science conferences in an attempt to convince people that there may be fossils on Mars.

Farmer explained to *Discover* magazine that Mars was once the great hope for finding life on another planet, noting that this was the whole point of the Viking mission in the 1970s. However, this proved to be a failure, because as Farmer points out, until now the search for life on other planets, known as exobiology, has concerned itself with trying to find live organisms. Farmer now maintains that a search for fossils is more likely to yield results.

Most researchers now believe that Mars as it is today would be unable to support life, but there is a consensus among astronomers that the planet was once a much hotter and wetter place, theoretically able to support life. Farmer now believes that as we

• The Martian landscape is an extremely inhospitable scene littered with volcanic activity.

are able to find fossils on Earth, dating 3.5 million years old, there is no reason to suggest that we cannot find fossils on Mars, probably dating from the same period. It is a widely held view that as life on Earth was evolving, it was entirely possible that the Martian climate and global environment was similar to Earth, and began to evolve at the same time. The problem is that Mars, unlike Earth, began to lose its heat-trapping atmosphere early on. Today, its water supply exists only as ice.

COULD THE FOSSIL BE CONTAMINATED?

Overshadowing the celebration about the discovery of life in the meteorite is the niggling doubt that the fossil may have been contaminated after entering the Earth's atmosphere or landing on the surface. Some ancient terrestrial life form may have worked its way into the rock, which would have been very hot indeed after its passage through the atmosphere, and then became trapped there as the rock cooled down.

Such contamination is possible, especially as the rock would have been on the surface of Antarctica for thousands of years, exposed to the elements. The suggestion of contamination has been ruled out by other researchers, who counter that although thousands of meteorites have been in Antarctica, there's never been a similar find.

MANY SCIENTISTS DO ACCEPT THAT LIFE ONCE EXISTED ON MARS, AS THE PLANET WAS ONCE A MUCH HOTTER AND WETTER PLACE

Adding to the controversy, scientists from the Open University of the UK recently claimed that evidence of life has also been found in a second Martian meteorite, believed to have left Mars 600,000 years ago and landed on Earth in 1979. Scientists found "significant amounts" of organic material, within the meteorite, believed to be 1.3 billion years old. Particularly exciting was the evidence of complex hydrocarbons – a kind of organic "soup" that is produced when living matter is subject to high temperatures and pressure. While the research into the meteorites is bound to rekindle the life on Mars debate, most scientists concur that any life on the Red Planet would be extremely basic – microscopic bacteria rather than advanced civilizations.

THE FACE OF MARTIAN CIVILIZATION?

Although the NASA space probe *Viking 1* failed to produce any conclusive evidence of life on Mars, one of its photographs, taken over the Cydonia region of the planet, did appear to reveal the outline of a face, one mile square, on the surface of Mars. NASA almost immediately dismissed the image as a "trick of light and shadow" but the Cydonia face continues to be the subject of intense interest from Ufologists who claim it is the relic of an ancient civilization. Another argument is that it is a schematic diagram, designed to be viewed from high above, that, along with nearby rocks, symbolizes Mars and its planets. While this may sound unlikely, Earth's ancient civilizations also left large symbolic imprints. Furthermore, NASA included a symbolic representation of Earth's place in the solar system and a drawing of a man and a woman, called the "Pioneer Plaque." Could it have been that an ancient Martian race created the Cydonia face in order to communicate with other intelligent life forms in a similarly symbolic way?

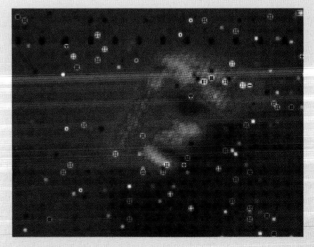

- As this image shows, the Cydonia face certainly looks like a humanoid visage. NASA insists it's a trick of the light; Ufologists believe it's a remnant of an ancient culture or representation of Mars and its moons.

MORE RECENT ENCOUNTERS: AREA 51 AND THE M-ZONE

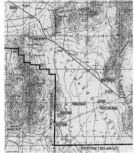

DREAMLAND, OR AREA 51 as it is better known, has to be one of the most notorious sites in Ufology. Area 51 is believed to be located inside the Groom Lake Air Force Base, just outside the small town of Rachel, Nevada, and the site is totally off-limits to the public. There was a time when a good view of the base could be had from the nearby Freedom Ridge mountain range, but the US military soon put a stop to the sightseeing by buying up the surrounding area. The most mystifying aspect of Area 51 is that the US government claims that it does not exist – a claim which, considering the amount of photographic evidence of a top-secret facility, is surprising.

The name Area 51 is derived from a grid map reference, and the Groom Lake Air Force Base has been in existence for at least 40 years. Millions of dollars have been spent in an attempt to keep Area 51's whereabouts from the general public, but nevertheless, it has become a mecca for UFO-minded tourists. For years, witnesses have claimed to have seen unknown lights perform breathtaking acts in the sky, stopping dead without any deceleration (as would be needed by conventional aircraft) and executing other baffling feats. Furthermore, lights have been seen to appear and disappear at will, and have even displayed the ability to change shape and intensity of hue.

Virtually every night around Area 51 you can find countless UFO enthusiasts with high-powered telescopes and binoculars, skywatching in the hope of catching a glimpse of these bizarre lights, despite the chances of being caught by the authorities. The entire base is surrounded by sophisticated camera surveillance equipment, able to read a car's plate from several miles away. Furthermore, the roads leading up to the base are littered with motion trackers which detect passing vehicles. The base's perimeter is subjected to constant patrol by security guards, commonly known as "Cammo Dudes" (this

- Despite spending millions of dollars trying to mask Area 51's identity, its supposed location has become a mecca for Ufologists and a moneyspinner for the local tourist industry. On any night, the vicinity is crowded with visitors hoping to see something unusual happening at Area 51 or in the sky. Some nearby houses have been taken over by Ufologists and bristle with the latest surveillance and radar equipment.

ONE OF THE MOST CONTROVERSIAL CLAIMS MADE BY UFOLOGISTS INVESTIGATING AREA 51'S ACTIVITIES, IS THAT IT'S BEING USED BY THE US MILITARY AS A STORAGE DEPOT FOR CRASHED ALIEN SPACECRAFT

name derives from their camouflage uniforms and unmarked four-wheel drives). Numerous warning signs can be seen, advising tourists to keep out; the penalty for ignoring the signs is a visit from the local sheriff, a fine and a night in the jail. However, the warning signs nearer the base's perimeter are even more threatening. They advise that crossing the boundary will mean entering a restricted area where the use of deadly force is authorized.

One of the most controversial claims made by Ufologists investigating Area 51's activities, is that it's being used by the US military as a storage depot for crashed alien spacecraft. The duties of the scientists and engineers who work on the base is to apply "back engineering" on these vehicles – in other words, to work out how the UFOs are powered, and then to calculate how this new-found knowledge could be used in the aerospace industry. This theory was popularized by Bob Lazar, who claims he was employed at

- Are crashed UFOs kept at Area 51 as Bob Lazar claims, or just the latest "Stealth" bombers.

PROJECT TWINKLE

Between 1948 and 1951, the state of New Mexico was visited by mysterious green fireballs with such alarming regularity that the US government eventually ordered a full-scale inquiry into the events, codenamed Project Twinkle.

The fireballs often buzzed civilian aircraft, including a USAF C-47 Dakota whose crew described the light as arcing towards them. This led to the assumption that the fireballs were not meteors, as no meteor could act as if under the control of a pilot. Project Twinkle was finally closed down in 1951, and in 1952 sightings of the fireballs ceased. The Project team never managed to find any trace of an impact point, and a satisfactory explanation for the sightings has never been broached.

the base as a propulsion system engineer working on a secret project between 1988 and 1990 codenamed Galileo. Lazar's claims have made him world-famous. He reckons that he worked on nine different recovered disks, kept at a section of the base known as S-4. These craft were housed in vast hangars built into the mountain side, and carefully camouflaged.

Lazar also claimed to have let slip details of his work to friends, who insisted that he took them to a vantage point at night to watch test flights of these fabulous craft. On one of these trips he claimed that he was captured by the security guards, who then escorted him to the base, where he was debriefed and threatened, before being released.

Many independent researchers have attempted to verify Lazar's story, and each time the official response has been that the base does not exist. He claims that he went public so the government would never dare kill him in revenge for speaking the truth about the base – such an assassination would merely validate his story.

Another mystery from Area 51 concerns the development of the "Stealth" aircraft. The US government is facing lawsuits from the families of several employees, who, it is claimed, suffered chemical poisoning from exposure to the substances used to create these silent planes. Area 51 is also the home of the world's longest runway – 6 miles – and regular flights arrive every day bringing in employees. The existence of the runway and many of the base's features have been confirmed by Russian satellite photographs.

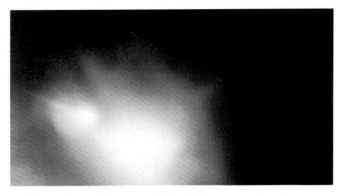

- These shots of luminous balls of lights were taken by villagers of Moljebka, near the Russian city of Perm. The large number of UFO phenomena reported around Moljebka, known as the "M-zone," has made the village world-famous. It appears to have been a major UFO hotspot since 1984.

- Area 51 expert Glenn Campbell is sure hi-tech aircraft are concealed at the base.

To this day, it is still not clear what Area 51 is being used for, and the authorities still stubbornly insist it doesn't even exist. If Lazar and Area 51 investigator Glenn Campbell are to be believed, then the strange lights regularly seen in the night skies over Rachel are the test flights of amazing new aircraft based on alien technology – although the lights could also be just regular flights of newly developed Stealth and Aurora aircraft, with absolutely no alien assistance whatsoever.

Whatever the real story behind Area 51, few places can offer the by-stander such spectacular sights on such a regular basis.

THE M-ZONE
Moving east, the remote village of

Moljebka, near Perm in the former Soviet Union, is becoming as famous among Ufologists as Area 51– especially with the thaw in East/West relations making it possible to visit this remarkable place. Moljebka appears to have been a UFO hot spot since 1984. As well as frequent sightings of luminous balls of light, claims are rife that UFOs have landed in the locality and that aliens have even been photographed. Regular expeditions are made to the "M-zone" in the hope of ascertaining further evidence. For decades it was forbidden to mention Ufology in the Soviet Union for fear of reprisals from the government. However, Russia's entire stance on the subject has shifted, and they are now one of the most open nations in regard to UFOs. The M-zone first became widely known in the West in 1989, as the Soviet regime crumbled. Yet it's long been famous in Russia for its continued UFO activity, including contacts with representatives of several alien civilizations.

6BC
BETHLEHEM, ISRAEL
THE GUIDING STAR
The Star of Bethlehem has long been believed by Ufologists to be more than just a star. Analysis of biblical reports suggest that the "star" was a controlled object able to stop and start, and apparently hover low over the site of the nativity to indicate its exact location to the three magi.

1235
KYOTO, JAPAN
FIRST UFO INVESTIGATION?
It's possible the first official UFO investigation took place near the Japanese city of Kyoto. On the night of 24th September, General Yoritsume and his army watched many unusual lights in the sky for some hours. A subsequent investigation speculated that the lights were stars "swaying in the wind."

1271
KAMAKURA, JAPAN
SAVED BY THE UFO
When the Buddhist priest Nichiren was about to be beheaded in Kamakura, near Tokyo, on 12th September 1271, an object appeared in the sky, similar to a full moon and very bright. The object was seen as a bad omen and Nichiren's execution was immediately called off.

1561
NUREMBERG, GERMANY
"FRIGHTFUL SPECTACLE"
The populace of the ancient German city of Nuremberg was treated to a a "frightful spectacle" on the morning of the 4th April, when strange lights and arrow-shaped objects infested the skies above their homes. Needless to say, these UFOs were regarded as a very bad omen.

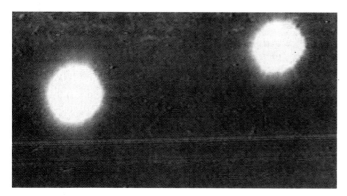

THE M-ZONE HAS NOW BECOME QUITE RENOWNED IN RUSSIA FOR ITS CONTINUED UFO ACTIVITY, INCLUDING CONTACTS WITH REPRESENTATIVES OF SEVERAL ALIEN CIVILIZATIONS

- Aliens or a photographic illusion? This is one of the most dramatic shots of alien entities from the M-zone. Careful analysis in Russia proves the photos have not been doctored.

THE DOWNING OF TWA FLIGHT 800

TWA 800 is an exceptional case in as much as it ended in tragedy, with all the passengers and crew killed in a terrifying mid-air explosion. The incident occurred near Long Island, New York, on 17th July 1996, and the media suggested that a bomb in the baggage compartment was responsible – although expert advice suggested that this was unlikely, unless the bomb actually detonated a fuel cell. It was also thought that a Stinger, a surface-to-air missile, had been launched, colliding with the plane and causing the explosion, but again there were faults with this line of reasoning. The first being that no party ever came forward to accept responsibility for the action, and again experts believed that a Stinger would not cause such widespread devastation. Yet there still remains another, even more disturbing possibility, namely that TWA Flight 800 collided with a UFO. Following the incident a number of eye-witnesses reported seeing a bright object hurtling toward the aircraft just seconds before it exploded. A couple in Johnston, Rhode Island, reported seeing a UFO 45 minutes before the explosion that downed the aircraft. This sighting was found to be only 70 airmiles from the vicinity where the TWA got into trouble.

More than 100 people claim to have seen the plane explode in mid-air, and out of these about 10% also reported seeing a second object, a bright light, racing towards the plane at the same time.

As a direct result of the eye-witness testimonies of streaking white lights, a third theory is now being put forward. This is that an errant meteor collided with the plane, an idea which is gaining momentum, especially after radar operators have now admitted that a second object was tracked shortly before the explosion.

1566

BASEL, SWITZERLAND
BLACK GLOBES FILLING THE SKY
A mass of strange globes was seen in the skies above the town of Basel, Switzerland, on 7th August 1566. The phenomenon was probably caused by a strange atmospheric occurrence rather than a visitation of alien craft. A mystery still unsolved to this day.

ATMOSPHERIC ENCOUNTERS

Ufology has reached a point where researchers are losing interest in the study of nocturnal lights. The reason seems to be that contact with aliens is felt to be a richer area of study, but another more plausible reason could well be that almost 99% of all sightings of unknown lights in the sky can be explained as atmospheric phenomena. Below are some of the rarer atmospheric conditions, some of which sound suspiciously like nocturnal lights.

The planet Venus, when viewed under certain conditions, can appear as a glowing orb that can give the illusion of an object moving in random patterns. Another strange atmospheric condition is a mock sun, or "sundog." This is caused by the sun's light reflecting an image of the sun onto shifting clouds, hence the name "mock sun." The moon can also appear as a most bizarre object, especially when it is close to the horizon, or when entering a cloud. It can even give the impression that it is hovering. On occasion the moon's light can shine on ice particles trapped in passing clouds, making the particles seem like shining, rounded objects in flight, an effect known as parhelia.

The phenomenon known as atokinesis can also confuse the untrained observer. This is when a star appears to move in a dark sky, sometimes even appearing to dart about erratically, very much like a glowing UFO. When this occurs, if a cloud obscures the star, it can make the star appear to shoot off at tremendous speed, or even blink out like a light bulb.

Lenticular clouds are formed in layers and can resemble a dome-shaped object, and are fairly well known, but a noctiluscent cloud is a different proposition altogether. These clouds are formed high up in the atmosphere, and are generally made up of ice particles and debris – and only visible at night. Because these clouds are at such great altitudes the sun's rays can reflect off them, even at night, causing the cloud to look like an eerie glowing purple object.

Finally, lightning can also be blamed for countless sightings of UFOs. The flashes of sheet lightning, for example, can mislead an observer into thinking that they are seeing a speeding extraterrestrial craft. Ball lightning and plasmoids are formed by electrified gas, which when burning, can vibrate, wobble and climb vertically. They can even be heard to give off a humming sound, which can be extremely frightening to the uninitiated.

- A classic UFO formation – or is it? These are in fact lenticular cloud formations over Santos, Brazil. Other weird effects can be created by noctiluscent clouds, which are formed high up in the atmosphere and are generally made up of ice particles and debris. The sun's rays reflect off noctiluscent clouds, making them look like glowing purple objects. Many, although not all, photos of lozenge or saucer-shaped UFOs turn out to be shots of clouds.

1881
MELBOURNE, AUSTRALIA
ROYAL APPARITION

On 11 June 1881, the then Princess of Wales was astonished to look out and see a "phantom vessel all aglow," while onboard a ship sailing from Melbourne to Sydney in Australia. The strange lights in the sky were also witnessed by a number of other crew members on the royal vessel.

1883 onwards
MARFA, TEXAS
MARFA LIGHTS

Odd lights began appearing over Marfa in 1883 and continue to be seen to the present day. They are described as balls of light which appear in the sky, change color and dance in the air. Skeptics claim the lights, which have also appeared in other parts of Texas, are just ball lightning or car headlights.

UFOs – From the Hollow Earth?

Since UFOs were first sighted, opinion has divided on where the craft actually come from. There are far too many theories for one chapter to cover, but the most popular claim is that aliens are dimensional travelers, able to warp the very structure of space, enabling them to use portals which can transport them vast distances in a matter of seconds. This theory has also been extended to suggest that "aliens" are actually fellow humans from our past and future, simply returning to give us advice.

For centuries, myths and legends have claimed that the earth is in fact hollow, and that an entirely alien subterranean race dwells below us. It is imagined that these races are highly developed and possess technology far more advanced than ours. There are many stories of underground civilizations and gateways to the underworld, but none are as staggering as the diary of Admiral Richard B. Byrd – Byrd claimed he not only saw the gateway to the underworld, but entered it and met its inhabitants.

On 19th February 1947, Byrd set off from his base camp in the Arctic for an epic exploratory flight over the North Pole. After only three hours into the flight he noticed below him a strange ice flow of a peculiar yellowish color. As he reduced his altitude for a better view, Byrd noticed that the coloration was

more bizarre than he had first thought, featuring reddish and purple hues. He also noticed a mountain range, which according to his maps, should definitely not have been there. After a further 29 minutes flight-time had elapsed, Byrd realized that the mountains were no illusion, and that they consisted of a series of small ranges that he'd never seen before. Even more surprisingly, he noticed that beyond the mountain range there was a green valley with a small stream running through it. He then claimed he saw a city ahead of him – by this time all the controls refused to respond, and the plane was acting as though buoyant. Off the port and starboard wings he saw an aircraft of an unknown origin with what appeared to be the Nazi swastika. The radio crackled and a voice was heard speaking in a slight Nordic or German accent: "Welcome, Admiral, to our domain, we shall land you in exactly seven minutes. Relax Admiral you are in good hands."

Byrd went on to describe the city as being a vast shimmering complex displaying beautiful colors. The inhabitants were described as very tall and blonde.

Byrd was granted an audience with the Master and told that they were a race known as the Arianni. They were concerned about the detonation of atomic weaponry, and had decided to send their flying machines, known as "The Fugelrads" to the surface to investigate. They had attempted to make contact with the surface dwellers, and had passed on their concerns, but had been ignored – their flying machines had even been pursued and fired at. The Master warned that the world was to come to an end, but some would survive, and after this the Arianni would come to the surface to teach humanity to start again. Byrd was told to return to the surface with the Master's warnings as a message, and he later passed it on to President Truman. The aviator claims he was sworn to silence by the Pentagon.

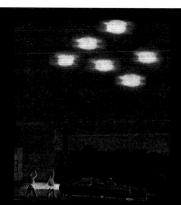

1913

Brazil
Long-Distance Lights

Over a number of months in 1913, a cluster of red and orange lights was seen traveling slowly and on a premeditated course, starting in Canada, and finishing in Brazil. The lights were described as "fiery," and they traveled in formation for the whole of the journey. No explanation has ever been found.

1930

New Mexico
Astronomical Sighting

In 1930, Clyde Tombaugh, the first astronomer to discover the planet Pluto, witnessed a group of six luminous elliptical objects in the sky, which completely baffled him. Tombaugh apparently made further sightings but chose not to mention them, out of fear it would undermine his professional credibility.

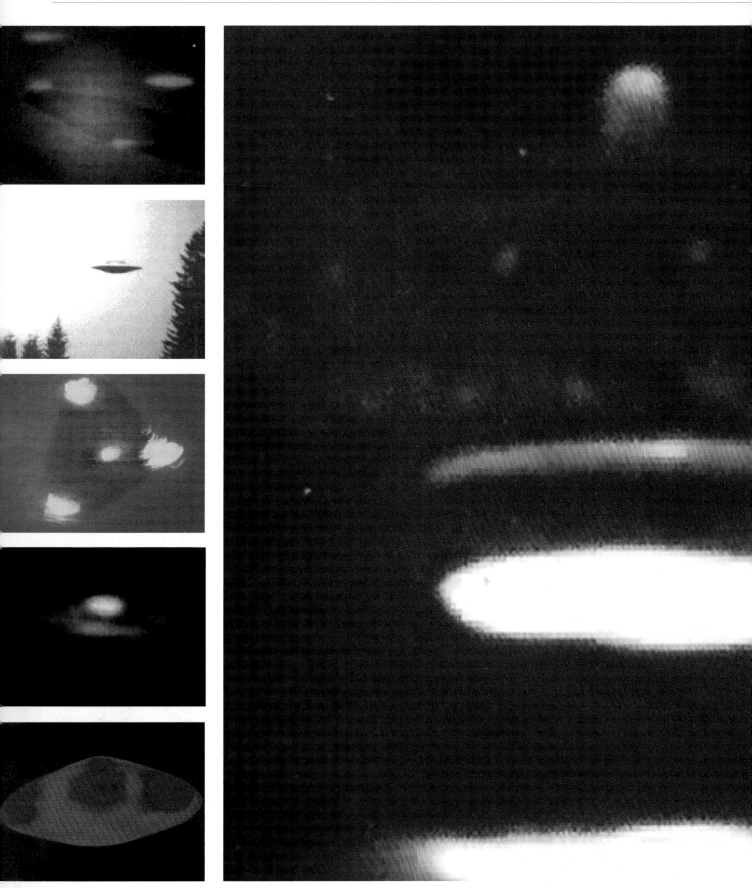

CHAPTER TWO

CLOSE ENCOUNTERS OF THE SECOND KIND

C LOSE ENCOUNTERS OF THE SECOND KIND ARE DEFINED AS a sighting of an object of unknown origin. This category encompasses objects seen in the sky or on the ground, and includes all the differing types of craft that have been observed and documented throughout history – such as cigar, egg, bell, saucer and triangular-shaped bodies.

Although the range of descriptions of UFOs is vast, the types of craft reported follow particular trends. When George Adamski revealed in 1952 that he had seen alien spaceships – and actually met Venusian pilots – he became famous worldwide. Adamski's revelation sparked an explosion of sightings similar in shape to the object he described, yet Adamski's bell-shaped UFO is rarely, if ever, reported today. Another popular craft much reported during this era was smooth and elongated – the cigar-shaped UFO.

Reportings of these archetypal saucer-shaped objects were all the rage in the 1940s and 1950s, especially after Kenneth Arnold's highly publicized 1947 sighting of nine flying saucers.

During the 1970s, elliptical or egg-shaped craft were often seen – again, physical characteristics that are rarely reported today. Even by the bizarre standards of Ufology, an egg or elliptical shape is curious. The reported craft were small, so small they would only be able to hold a couple of passengers. This gave rise to speculation that these objects were only scout craft, launched by much larger motherships.

Throughout the 1980s there were reports of a new type of craft – not so much new in shape, but certainly new in terms of maneuverability and speed. The era was kicked off by Ed Walters' sightings in Gulf Breeze, Florida. The startling photographic evidence (which comprises over 40 images) captured by Walters shows a highly illuminated object moving at fantastic speeds – the craft looks like a mix between the classic saucer shape and the earlier Adamski craft.

The 1990s are characterized by sightings of a radically new object: the flying triangle or wedge-shaped UFO. Sightings of similarly shaped objects are currently being reported all over the world – the most famous incident being the recent Belgian UFO scare in which more than 13,500 people reported seeing a triangular-shaped craft over a 12-month period.

HISTORICAL SIGHTINGS

WHILE IT'S WIDELY BELIEVED THAT THE roots of Ufology only extend as far back as Kenneth Arnold's 1947 sightings of a UFO flotilla, there's compelling evidence that man has witnessed UFOs since time immemorial. The Bible, for instance, has accounts of clouds that mysteriously move through the sky, guiding the way for their followers. These clouds stop at night, often illuminating the surrounding area, and continue to guide followers in the morning. The fact that these objects seem to be acting in a controlled manner would indicate they are piloted, or even remotely controlled. One of the most fascinating sightings in the Old Testament was witnessed by the priest Ezekiel, who not only described the landing of a huge UFO, but may also have been treated to a ride in it. The description as given in the Old Testament (Chapter 1:1-21) is very graphic.

> AND I LOOKED, AND, BEHOLD, A WHIRLWIND CAME OUT OF THE NORTH, AND A FIRE INFOLDING ITSELF, AND A BRIGHTNESS WAS ABOUT IT, AND OUT OF THE MIDST THEREOF AS THE COLOR OF AMBER, OUT OF THE MIDST OF THE FIRE.

This is widely believed to be one of the first written descriptions of a landing UFO. The whirlwind would be the immense downdraft caused by the object's thrusters, while "the fire infolding itself" is the perfect description of a rocket's

- Pilot Kenneth Arnold observed nine boomerang-shaped craft flying over the Cascade mountains in Washington on 24th June 1947 – many people incorrectly believe this to be the start of UFO sightings. Historic books and documents provide a different story.

- How do you describe a UFO if you've never seen an airplane? The Book of Ezekiel (Chapter 1:1-21) in the Old Testament has been interpreted by many Ufologists as being early evidence for the existence of alien craft. Regardless of the interpretation, the texts of Ezekiel (opposite) continue to enthuse UFO followers and baffle theologians.

10,000BC
NIAUX, FRANCE
CAVE PAINTING
Ever since the dawn of time alien visitations have been recorded. Cave paintings etched by prehistoric man depict traditional hunting scenes interspersed with random images of glowing men wearing goldfish bowl-like helmets. The most striking of these can be found in Niaux, France.

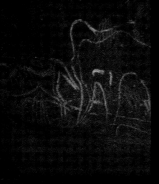

7000BC
NEPAL
LOLLADOFF PLATE
The Lolladoff plate is a startling discovery which was found in Nepal. The plate appears to show a disk-shaped object in the centre (which has been likened to a UFO), and a small creature around the outside, resembling a Grey alien. Astonishingly, the plate is around 4000 years old.

800BC
GUATEMALA, MEXICO
RETURN OF THE STAR PEOPLE
According to Mayan prophesy, the 1990s would herald the return of the "star people" that supposedly visited the ancient race. While the star people haven't made definite contact yet, Mexico is one of today's current UFO hot spots and yields some of the most spectacular photographic evidence.

- Ancient philosophers such as Aristotle (right) wrote of anomalous objects in the sky which we would now classify as UFO sightings. In the pre-scientific age, UFOs and other paranormal phenomena were widely regarded as messages from the Gods rather than evidence of beings from other galaxies.

	GEOMETRIC		CODEX
PIKTUN (20 BAK'TUNOB)			
BAK'TUN (20 K'ATUNOB)			
K'ATUN (20 TUNOB)			
TUN (18 WINALOB)			
WINAL (20 K'INOB)			
K'IN (1 DAY)			

- Mayan hieroglyphic writing is made up of symbols that represent whole words or syllables consisting of consonant/vowel pairs or vowels. In syllabic writing, words are spelled out by signs ordered within glyph blocks. Many believe ancient Mayan texts hold the secrets to the race's advanced technology, and that the technology came from beyond this planet.

boosters flaming in order to keep the craft true during its descent. Later in the chapter, Ezekiel describes the emergence of four living creatures. Yet Zechariah Sitchin speculates in his book *Divine Beings* that these were probably not living, breathing biological entities at all, but small, all-terrain landcraft. Ezekiel mentions that as he beheld the living creatures, one wheel was placed upon the earth. The prophet later confirms there was a wheel within a wheel – possibly his attempt to describe a tire. This and other intriguing descriptions from the Bible, not to mention other ancient texts such as those of the Mayan civilization of South America, has led to the development of the Ancient Astronaut Theory – a hypothesis supported by Sitchin and Erich von Däniken, author of *Chariots of the Gods*.

Gods from the Stars
Old Testament aside, other ancient texts describe gods who came from the stars. The Incas, for

THE MAYANS POSSESSED GREAT TECHNICAL KNOWLEDGE, AMAZINGLY ADVANCED FOR THEIR DAY, THAT AGAIN WOULD IMPLY EXTRATERRESTRIAL CONTACT HAD BEEN MADE

example, believed that the galaxy was inhabited by divine beings. Meanwhile the Mayans possessed great technical knowledge – amazingly advanced for their day – that some scholars attribute to extra-terrestrial contact. The most convincing evidence for the visitation of UFOs, as far back as 10,000 years ago, can be found in the Indian epic the *Mahabharrata*.

Within the *Mahabharrata*, the longest religious text ever written, are numerous mentions of *Vimanas* or

216BC
Rome, Italy
Ships over Italy
Julius Obsequens, a Roman writer, claimed in his work **The Prodigia** that "things like ships" were seen in the sky over Italy in 216BC. The "ships" made another appearance in 215BC. According to a German manuscript from the 16th century, the phenomena appeared again in 170BC.

200BC
Mali
Nommo Contact Tribe
The Dogon Tribe of Mali strongly believe that they were taught all of their cultural ways by a breed of amphibious peoples from the Sirius star system. This race of beings were called the Nommo. It is undeniable that the Dogon have an understanding of Sirius that defies logical explanation.

7BC
Judea
Star of Bethlehem
The Star of Bethlehem is believed by many Ufologists to have been an alien craft guiding the three wise men to the birth site of Jesus. This claim appears to be corroborated by the erratic movements of the star, which acted as though under some form of intelligent control, guiding the magi to the Nativity.

OF EVEN GREATER SIGNIFICANCE ARE THE SIGHTINGS OF CICERO, ANCIENT ROME'S GREATEST HISTORIAN WRITING IN THE 1ST CENTURY BC. ON ONE OCCASION HE OBSERVED THE SUN AT NIGHT

flying machines. These flying machines came in a variety of designs and sizes, and, according to the ancient text, were fuelled by quicksilver. Vimanas, which could perform complex aerial acrobatics and travel at astonishing speeds, were used to transport the gods of that era.

Other civilizations to describe strange aerial objects include the Ancient Greeks, Egyptians and the Romans. The Greek philosopher Aristotle wrote of "heavenly disks" as early as 4BC, going on to claim that a meteor that fell out of the sky at Aegospotami "rose up in the wind and descended elsewhere." Hardly the conventional behavior of a meteor, even allowing for Aristotle's poetic license. Moving forward to 66BC, the Roman scientist and historian Pliny recorded that "a spark fell from a star and descended to the earth until it was the size of the moon." At this point the spark stopped dead and hovered in the air for a while.

Of even greater significance are the sightings of Cicero, Ancient Rome's greatest historian

- Alexander the Great wrote of inexplicable flying objects assisting in his siege of the city of Tire in 322BC. Several years before, he witnessed two silver shields diving at his troops as they crossed the Jaxartes river on the border of India.

- Marcus Tullius Cicero – one of Ancient Rome's greatest historians – may not have realized he witnessed unidentified flying phenomena when he claimed to have observed the sun at night split open to reveal several unusual spherical objects.

writing in the 1st century BC. On one occasion he observed the sun at night, an astonishing sight which was accompanied by loud noises. After this the sun appeared to split open, revealing several unusual spherical objects. Cicero's compatriot, the historian Livy, also viewed strange phenomena. He reported "phantom ships that gleamed in the sky," and even more curiously, an "altar" which appeared to be surrounded by men in white clothing. This phenomenon was also seen in Hadria, near Venice, in 214BC.

ALEXANDER'S ENCOUNTERS
Alexander the Great even seems to have been assisted in his campaigns by extraterrestrial intervention. Some of the most bizarre of Alexander's sightings come in the account of the siege of the city of Tire in 322BC. Apparently, a triangular formation of five "round silver shields" circled the city, eventually aiding Alexander's forces by destroying the city walls with beams of light. Yet this was not the first of Alexander's

1254
ST. ALBANS, ENGLAND
COLORED SHIP SIGHTED
Chronicler Matthew of Paris curiously recorded that at midnight "in serene sky and clear air, with stars shining and the moon eight days old, there suddenly appeared in the sky a kind of large ship elegantly shaped, well equipped and of marvellous color." So goes his bizarre story...

1528
UTRECHT, HOLLAND
CROSS IN THE SKY
The chronicler Wolffart reported that a "strange and cruel sight was seen in the sky" during the siege of the Dutch city of Utrecht. Apparently an object in the shape of a Burgundian cross appeared over the city, described as "yellow in color and fearful to behold."

1561
NUREMBURG, GERMANY
BALLS OF LIGHT
An extremely frightening spectacle occurred on this day early in the morning which had many people glued to the sky: an inexplicable aerial display of tube-shaped objects and balls of light. The chilling account was later depicted in a haunting woodcutting by witness Hans Glaser.

1878
TEXAS
FLYING SAUCER COINED
Contrary to popular belief, the term "flying saucer" was coined 70 years before Kenneth Arnold was reported as saying it. John Martin used the phrase to describe his sighting of an object about the size of an orange which grew in size until directly overhead, after which it looked more like a saucer.

encounters with alien craft. In 329BC he witnessed an aerial display of two silver shields repeatedly diving at his troops as they tried to cross the Jaxartes river on the border of India. These encounters certainly did no harm to Alexander's claims that he was semi-divine, being the offspring of an Egyptian deity and an earth mother.

Fierce disapproval of the whole concept of aliens by the early Christian church meant that reportings of UFOs during the medieval era were scant. Indeed, it wasn't until the late 1800s that a new rash of unexplained sightings was recorded.

Jumping forward to the 20th century, both German and Allied fighter planes were buzzed by "Foo Fighters" at the end of the Second World War. Pilots claimed that Foo Fighters could travel at the same speed as conventional fighters, but if challenged, would roar away at speeds far beyond 1940s aviators. Each side thought the other had developed an amazingly fast prototype aircraft: yet even many years after the war, no-one has ever admitted responsibility for the Foo Fighters.

- The term "Foo Fighters" is derived from a comic-book phrase: "where there's foo, there's fire."

UFOs Over Egypt

As a civilization with a keen interest in the paranormal, it's not surprising that ancient Egyptians also recorded encounters with UFOs. In 1450 BC, Pharaoh Thutmosis III ordered the official recording of the following sighting.

"In the year 22 (of the Pharaoh's reign), of the third month of winter, sixth hour of the day, the scribes of the House of Life found that there was a circle of fire coming from the sky. It had no head. From its mouth came a breath that stank. One rod long was its body and a rod wide, and it was noiseless. And the hearts of the scribes became terrified and confused, and they laid themselves flat on their bellies. They reported to the Pharaoh ... Now after some days had gone by, behold these things became more numerous in the skies than ever. They shone more than the brightness of the sun, and extended to the limits of the four supports of the heavens. Dominating in the sky was the station of these fire circles. The army of Pharaoh looked on with him in their midst. Thereupon the fire circles ascended higher in the sky towards the south. Fishes and winged animals or birds fell from the sky. A marvel never before known since the foundation of this land. And Pharaoh caused incense to be brought to make peace on earth ... And what happened was ordered by Pharaoh to be written in the annals of the House of Life, so that it be remembered forever."

So runs a baffling account of aerial phenomena that still has

the power to haunt modern readers. Whatever the Pharaoh observed does not conform to any meteorological or atmospheric occurrence known to mankind.

1891
Crawfordsville, Indiana
Headless Monster
Two icemen working in Crawfordsville, Indiana, in late September of 1891 described seeing what they termed a "seemingly headless monster" propelled by fin-like attachments. The phenomenon was said to be 20 feet long and 8 feet wide. And airborne...

1896
California
Californian Airship
The first reports of the great American wave of airship sightings took place in California, where witnesses described an object with a dark body above a brilliant light.

MODERN DAY CE2S

ONE OF THE MORE REGRETTABLE SIDE effects of the computer age is the ease with which photographic evidence can be faked. Indeed, accusations of falsehood continue to dog one of the best-documented cases of UFO sightings of recent times.

In the latter part of the 1980s Ed Walters, a property developer and resident of Gulf Breeze, Florida, became an overnight celebrity when the media got a glimpse of some of the spectacular UFOs he had photographed. Walters's photos depicted lavishly-illuminated crafts hovering over roadsides, only a few feet off the ground, beaming down shafts of light to the road below. These craft often only appeared to Walters, and he managed to capture many of them on film.

For a long time the Gulf Breeze sightings were hailed as the best case for the existence of UFOs, yet the excitement soon turned to doubt. It was later revealed that during a routine interview with Ed Walters led by members of MUFON (Mutual UFO Network), a scale-model UFO was discovered in his basement.

Walters's story was that he had simply tried to build a model of one of the UFOs he saw, but his explanation was discounted, his credibility ruined, and the whole area of Gulf Breeze declared of no interest to UFO watchers – disappointing, as many well-documented sightings had originated from the region long before Walters's claims, and continue to be reported on a regular basis.

THE BELGIAN TRIANGLE

Beginning December 1989, many Belgians began reporting unusual aerial activities by strange triangular-shaped objects. Within a year, more than 13,500 reports of a bizarre wedge-shaped object had flooded in from a wide spectrum of people, including air force pilots, police officers and radar operators. Belgium's skies seemed to be infested by strange objects, which many believed to be of alien origin. Fortunately, photographic and video evidence abounds. One of the most famous photos of the Belgian Triangle depicts a wedge-shaped craft with a light at either corner of its triangular body.

At the time, the shape was unfamiliar to civilians. Unfamiliar, at least, until the recent announcement of the Waverider or Loflyte. The Waverider is a joint NASA and USAF project, and can be crudely described as a triangular-shaped aircraft that can fly at up to five times the speed of sound. In light of this announcement, many UFO investigators are starting to believe that the Waverider, or a prototype model, was responsible for the mass sightings. Skeptics believe the timing of the Waverider's announcement to be suspicious, and part of an involved cover-up.

Belgium was not the only nation to find its skies infested with this object. Indeed, the flying triangle has been reported in nearly every country – although some countries, such as the UK, do appear to have a higher concentration of incidents. The most memorable sighting of the flying triangle was reported in Telford, Shropshire, by hotel worker John Doran on 26 December 1995. Doran was traveling in his car to work when he noticed a light through the trees that lined the roadside. At first he believed the light to be coming from one of the few farmhouses situated along the Wrekin

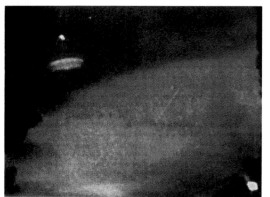

● Two of the 40-plus pictures Ed Walters claims to have taken of UFOs in the Gulf Breeze area of Florida during the 1980s. The images have since been discounted by members of MUFON (Mutual UFO Network) since the discovery of a model UFO in Walters's basement and the dismissal of his subsequent explanation. Despite this, independent UFO sightings continue to occur in the area.

- Is this image, photographed over Belgian skies, the recently-announced joint NASA and USAF project dubbed Waverider or LoFlyte? If it is, why have the two agencies claimed that no prototype exists yet? And if it isn't, what is this craft that has been witnessed by 13,500 people and has been involved in several near-miss incidents?

- This startling representation of a flying triangle was painted by a UFO witness in Farnborough, England. She claims that the object often lands at a nearby Ministry of Defence base but is never seen leaving. She believes it's stored there.

TRIANGULAR UFO SIGHTED IN BELGIUM

All the Belgian sightings, which began around December 1989, were either at dusk or in the middle of the night. The first thing to be seen against the dark sky was a triangular formation of blinking lights. The reports conclude that the craft was approximately 200 feet wide and could fly and hover as low as 300 feet off the ground. The only noise ever reported was a very gentle humming. F-16 fighters were twice scrambled in response to the sheer number of reports from the public. For example, on 30th March 1990 at 11pm, the master controller of the Air Defense radar at Glons picked up an object and recorded it traveling at an altitude of 10,000 feet. At 11:50 pm another radar station started to monitor the object. Two F-16s were scrambled from Beauvelain Airbase and set a course for the UFO with the guidance of the Glons radar station. A total of nine interceptions were attempted, but the erratic behavior of the UFO made interception impossible. Four police stations on the night also reported seeing the object.

mountain range. But as he drove on he noticed that the light formed a perfect triangle in the sky. When Doran got to work, he immediately alerted the other kitchen staff, who rushed outside to peer at the sky. The object hung silently in the sky before eventually moving off towards nearby Shawbury. What's particularly fascinating is during subsequent investigations of this sighting, researchers separated the witnesses and asked each one to draw a representation of the

- Nick Pope, ex-UK defense official, thinks the Belgian UFOs are a security threat.

object. All drew a similar craft, with similar coloring. These flying triangles seem able to fly at tremendous speeds, evade radar, hover silently for long periods of time, and literally run rings around conventional aircraft sent to intercept them. Such tactics have convinced Nick Pope, a former member of the British Ministry of Defence's UFO Reporting Section, that the triangular UFOs represent a real aerial threat and should be treated as hostile until a reasonable explanation is broached.

UFO Fiesta in Brazil

Brazil is another country that's witnessed more than its fair share of Close Encounters of the Second Kind. Some truly startling cases have surfaced in this

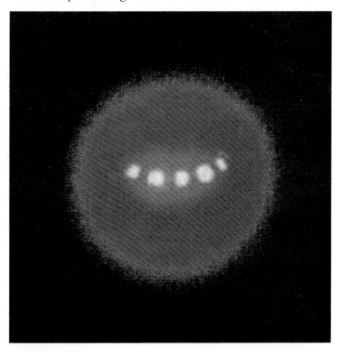

country, the following being a small selection. On the night of 16th August 1995, truck driver Louis Carlos was traveling in his vehicle when a large ball of light came up behind him.

He first spotted the light in his rear-view mirror, and despite speeding away in the hope of outrunning the object, it kept pace with his truck. It even struck the vehicle at one point. On that same evening another truck driver saw the same object. He reported that his steering wheel suddenly became too hot to handle, and the vehicle began to malfunction while the interior of the truck become unbearably hot. The driver was too scared to leave the stifling cabin as it would have meant coming face to face with his mysterious pursuer.

ONE OF THE MOST ASTOUNDING CHARACTERISTICS OF MEXICAN UFO SIGHTINGS IS THE ANNUAL APPEARANCE ON THAT NATION'S INDEPENDENCE DAY

On another occasion, several soldiers based at a military camp saw two bowl-shaped objects approaching from different parts of the sky. The objects joined together in mid-air and formed a much larger solid metallic orb. One of the most convincing sightings took place in 1986. No less than 21 balls of light, each 300 feet in diameter, flew over San Reno. They were detected by radar and Mirage jets were launched to investigate. Other commercial pilots and eye-witnesses on the ground saw the UFO fly by. The 21 UFOs were officially recorded, and for once the Defense Ministry admitted the event took place. It has been estimated by leading Brazilian Ufologist A. J. Gevaerd that at least 50% of Brazilians have witnessed a UFO.

Moving north into Central America, Mexico is another nation rich in UFO lore. Mexico's skies

- Two shots of UFOs taken in Brazil, spanning almost 40 years. The bottom shot was taken in Barra da Tijuca, on 7th May 1952, while the top image dates from the early 1990s. Brazil remains a major world UFO hotspot.

- An artist's impression of the red lights that appear over Brazil on a regular basis. Some 21 balls of light flew on San Reno, each 300 feet in diameter.

● Curious video footage recently shot which depicts Unidentified Flying Objects over Mexico. As predicted by the Mayans, Mexico would see a return of the star people in the 1990s. Regardless of the Mayan prophecies, Mexico is currently being subjected to a spate of inexplicable aerial sightings. There is much compelling video and photographic evidence to support the case for the existence of UFOs.

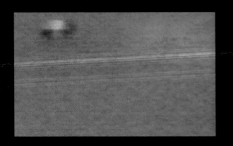  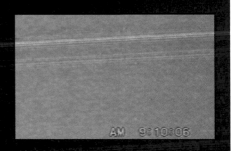

appear to be swarming with UFOs at present, as appears to have been predicted by the Mayan civilization around 800BC. Sightings have mushroomed in recent years, with as many as 20 objects being seen in the sky at the same time on more than one occasion. Even TV crews have begun to skywatch in the hope of that elusive footage that will stun audiences worldwide.

One of the most astounding characteristics of Mexican UFO sightings is the annual appearance on the nation's Independence Day. On 14th September, the skies above Mexico City appear to play host to formations of UFOs. This has become such a regular occurrence, happening for the last four years, that researchers from around the world gather on this occasion in the hope of capturing a UFO on camera. Mexican Carlos Diaz is just one of the observers who has photographed some absolutely amazing sights. Amongst his most famous pictures is a sequence of shots showing enormous glowing orange balls of light. Diaz reports that the globes appeared to have a life of their own. Diaz is quite a personality in the UFO world, also claiming to be in regular contact with aliens.

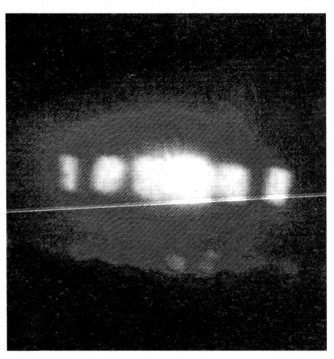

● Mexico's Carlos Diaz has taken spectacular shots of UFOs which emit bright light, are reported as being able to flicker in and out of view, and travel at tremendous speed. Mexican radio towers scan the skies for further evidence.

● South America is one of the world's major UFO hot spots. This image together with countless others form part of the ever-growing evidence for UFOs. On 14th September, Mexico's Independence Day, sightings of UFOs are regularly reported.

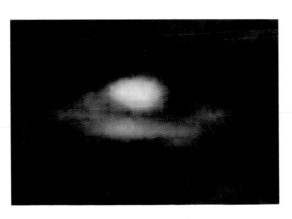 

STRANGE LIGHTS IN THE FOREST

SOME OF THE MOST REMARKABLE Close Encounters of the Second Kind have occurred in Britain's wooded glades and forests. At the best of times these can be intimidating places, but add to the already sinister atmosphere the zest of unexplained alien phenomena and you have a recipe for a captivating enigma worthy of *The X Files*.

The events associated with a modest plantation of pine trees 8 miles north-east of the town of Ipswich are now seen as the most important UFO encounter ever to occur in the UK. The profile of the case and its proximity to several USAF-administered air bases give it global significance, second only to the Roswell incident of 1947.

A strange object heading from the sea towards the Woodbridge and Bentwaters USAF bases was tracked on radar in the early hours of 27th December 1980. As soon as the object was picked up by radar, Woodbridge and Bentwaters assumed a state of full alert.

For a while there was complete confusion as none of the staff were sure what they were dealing with. According to some reports, a bright ball of light seemed to crash into nearby Rendelsham Forest. A patrol was promptly dispatched to the vicinity. As the patrol approached the area, they came across a locked farm gate, and were forced to continue their search on foot. From the gate, a narrow path led directly to the forest.

HOVERING OBJECT

The servicemen followed the path for approximately half a mile and then stumbled upon a clearing, where to their amazement, they saw a conical metallic object hovering above them. The object, whatever it was, appeared to be suspended in a haze of yellow mist, through which one of the men recalls seeing the vague outline of triangular-shaped landing gear. As the men looked up, they could see a pulsating beam of light emitting a rotating circle of red and blue light around the perimeter of the object. It was obviously fully aware of the servicemen's presence and began to back away. Not wanting to lose sight of the object, the airmen

- When the strange hovering object became aware of the presence of humans, it began to back off.

followed it and eventually came close enough for one of them to actually climb on top of the object and confirm it was physically solid. By this time, the growing unreality of the situation was making the patrol members behave irrationally. At least one of them had to be forcibly dragged from the forest after falling into a trance-like condition, and the others were left in a highly confused state of mind.

At this point, the sequence of events becomes slightly confused. Various accounts by eyewitnesses speak of strange lights that continued to plague the vicinity throughout the night and of a peculiar-shaped craft landing in the woods and small creatures with domed heads being seen to emerge. Apparently, the craft remained on the ground long enough to be approached by Base Commander Gordon Williams, who is said to have attempted to communicate with the aliens using sign language. An eye-witness claimed that the beings – possibly robots – were carrying out repairs to the craft which appeared to have sustained damage whilst descending through the trees.

AN EYE-WITNESS CLAIMED THAT THE BEINGS – POSSIBLY ROBOTS – WERE CARRYING OUT REPAIRS TO THE CRAFT WHICH APPEARED TO HAVE SUSTAINED DAMAGE WHILST DESCENDING THROUGH THE TREES

Once these repairs were complete, the aliens were observed taking off again in a brilliant burst of light. The following day, the whole site was subjected to intense investigation. Small indentations, thought to have been where the landing legs stood, emitted above normal levels of radiation. In addition,

- In addition to the mysterious lights and UFOs, there were also reports of odd humanoid figures in the woods.

- Folklore has it that animals, and even a priest, have disappeared near the woods. Were aliens responsible?

overhead branches and leaves were torn away and parted as if some massive object had plunged through the trees. During that night, there were strange reports that local farm animals and domestic pets had become panicky and frightened for no apparent reason.

Predictably, the authorities attempted to cover up the whole episode, but the extent of the incident, and the fact that there were civilian witnesses, made this almost impossible. The incident was further confused by the release of a moment-by-moment tape-recording of the foot search through the pine woods. This was of a highly dramatic nature, and most Ufologists have always doubted its authenticity. It is also widely believed that the entire episode was filmed on video by a USAF officer, but no footage has ever been publicly released – so far.

COLLIDING WITH A UFO

● On the left, pilot Kenji Terauchi shows a drawing of the craft he saw over Alaska. On the right, a Canadian-Pacific crew show a sketch of the UFO that paced them briefly over South America.

THE RECENT spate of UFO sightings in Mexico reinforce the fact that UFOs seem to have a great deal of interest in commercial air traffic. This interest has led to several life-threatening situations, as the objects have come very close to the aircraft. A good example of this occurred on 28th July 1994, when the following conversation was recorded between the control tower and a pilot:

Pilot: This is Mexican 180, what traffic do you have on radar? I have an unidentified object on my right moving very fast.
Tower: There's nothing on radar.
Pilot: You have nothing on radar. What do we do?
Tower: Maintain altitude and heading.

Later on, another flight was on its final approach to the airport in Mexico City when a UFO almost caused a cataclysmic mid-air disaster. The pilot, Captain Raymundo Cervantes Ruano, heard a loud bang as he was lowering the plane's landing gear. The following conversation was recorded between Ruano and the control tower:

Pilot: What was that?
Co-Pilot: I don't know.
Pilot: Check the lamp and the door. Tower, we have an emergency!
Tower: You've had a collision.

The subsequent investigation showed that Flight 129 had indeed collided with a UFO and further maintenance checks showed that the aircraft's shock absorbers had been torn off. Radar control also confirmed that they had two unidentified objects on the screens at the time Flight 129 radioed in with an emergency.

Flight 129 was carrying 109 passengers and a full-scale tragedy was only narrowly averted. Even more harrowing is the fact that this was not an isolated incident; as many as two mid-air UFO encounters are reported by pilots every week. And it is not only the danger of collision that is concerning the authorities.

1942
NEWBIGGIN ON SEA, ENGLAND
FIRST BRITISH ABDUCTION?
Private Albert Lancashire, armed with nothing more than a rifle, was guarding a radar base on the North Sea coast when a light appeared in the sky apparently throwing a beam from the rim of a round object. The beam shone in his face. After experiencing floating sensations, Lancashire passed out.

1946
YUKON, OKLAHOMA
FLYING BATHTUBS
A salesman passing through Yukon, Oklahoma, reported seeing six strange objects in the sky at dusk. "They appeared as large as washtubs, and were very high up, flying in formation and at an incredible speed".

1947
RICHMOND, VIRGINIA
TRACKED SILVER DISK
Meteorological staff were tracking a weather balloon with a theodolite when they noticed a silver disk-shaped object with a large dome on its surface crossing the sky. The object was much larger than the balloon, and disappeared from view after just 15 seconds. The sighting remains a mystery.

It has now been suggested that UFOs also interfere with the aircraft's onboard computers, resulting in false altitude and directional read-outs which may well lead to a fatal accident. Pilots are therefore determined that their mysterious mid-air encounters are not just hushed up.

Alien craft often appear as part of aerial fly-bys, as happened in Mexico on the Independence Day celebrations of 16th September 1991. More than 20 helicopters flew in close formation as part of a show of military strength; joining them was a small metallic object which glided ahead of and just under the helicopters, seemingly oblivious of any dangers of collision. Much video footage has been recorded together with photographic evidence to back up the claims that Mexico is rapidly becoming one of the world's leading UFO hot spots.

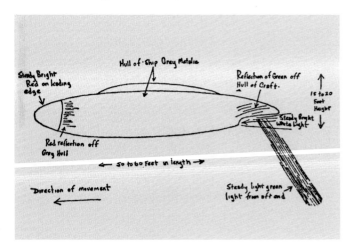

- A sketch of the UFO seen over Ohio by helicopter pilot Captain Lawrence J. Coyne on 18th October 1973. What's remarkable about Coyne's drawing is the amount of detail it reveals, especially as the pilot was controlling a chopper at the same time as he was trying to remember all the details of this anomalous cigar-shaped craft.

VOLCANIC PHENOMENON

Another fascinating account of a UFO sighting in Mexico was reported around the volcano Popcatepteptl, long considered to be dormant. Air traffic control had been tracking objects to and from the volcano for over three years and eventually, following a spate of heavy UFO activity in this area, an investigation was mounted. It was discovered that the volcano was far from dormant, and was, in fact, showing signs of imminent activity. In February 1994, the volcano began to smoke, and in December of that year Popcatepteptl erupted violently, covering the city of Puebla with ash. Fortunately, a full-scale evacuation of the city meant that many thousands of lives were saved. People never lost sight of the fact that it was the heavy UFO presence that originally drew the investigative team to the volcano, leading some to regard the UFOs as some kind of savior.

Many people in Mexico are now pointing to even stronger evidence written hundreds of years ago as proof that the "Star Travelers" would return when they did, in 1991. The Mayans, an ancient Mexican civilization, wrote many prophecies and one reads as follows: "In the era of the sixth sun all that was buried will be discovered, truth shall be the seed of life and the sons of the sixth sun will be the ones who travel through the stars."

This has been proven to have great relevance to the current Mexican wave of sightings because the "sixth sun" refers to the total solar eclipse in 1991, during which four identical metallic UFOs were spotted in the cities of Puebla, Mexico City and Tepyeji. This solar eclipse would have been the Mayan's sixth sun signifying a new era, the era of truth.

1947
MANITOU SPRINGS, COLORADO
DANCING OBJECTS
Between 12:15 pm and 1:15 pm on 19th May, a silvery object was seen approaching Manitou Springs. It halted and remained motionless in the sky for some minutes before performing a number of complex aeronautics. It finally rose and shot off at incredible speed, unlike any conventional aircraft of the era.

1947
WASHINGTON STATE
DISK OBJECTS SIGHTED
This sighting occurred on the same day as Kenneth Arnold's more famous one. Prospector Fred Johnson was on the Cascade Mountain range when he saw a strange reflection in the sky and grabbed his telescope. Johnson described six disk-shaped objects which apparently made no noise.

1947
ROSWELL, NEW MEXICO
UFO CRASH SITE
This apparent crash landing of a UFO has gone down in folklore and is still the subject of wide and heated debate. A UFO is said to have come down on the ranch of Mac Brazel and alien bodies recovered. Many witnesses reported seeing a big glowing object on the day in question.

ASTRONAUTS GIVE THEIR EVIDENCE

OF ALL THE EVIDENCE FOR THE EXISTENCE of UFOs, none can be more compelling than the evidence given by trained observers, such as pilots, military personnel and of course, astronauts.

Over the last two decades many top astronauts have begun to speak out about what they really saw in space on various lunar missions.

Major Gordon Cooper was one of the original Mercury astronauts and one of the last Americans to make a solo space flight. But it was on 15th May 1963, when he went into space via a Mercury capsule for a 22-orbit mission around the globe, that he saw a UFO way out in space. On the last orbit, Cooper reported seeing a glowing greenish object ahead of him, quickly approaching his capsule. He reported his sighting to the Muchea tracking station, near Perth in Australia. The object was picked up by the tracking station's radar, and therefore presumed to be a very real, solid vehicle.

The whole incident was reported

• Solo astronaut Major Gordon Cooper saw a UFO far out in space.

by NBC television who were tracing the mission stage by stage, but when Cooper landed, the NBC reporters were told not to ask the astronaut about his sighting.

This was not the first time Cooper had come face to face with an unidentified flying object. In 1951, whilst flying an F-86 Sabrejet over western Germany, he encountered metallic saucer-shaped disks at considerable altitude which seemed to have the ability to out-maneuver his aircraft. Major Cooper has also testified before the United Nations, stating: "I believe that these extraterrestrial vehicles and their crews are visiting this planet from other planets, and that most astronauts are reluctant to discuss UFOs. I did have occasions in 1951 to have two days of observation of many flights of them, of different sizes flying in fighter formation, generally from east to west over Europe."

It is also believed that Major Cooper made the following comments while being taped, although the recording's authenticity has never been established.

FOR MANY YEARS I HAVE LIVED WITH A SECRET, IN A SECRECY IMPOSED ON ALL SPECIALISTS IN ASTRONAUTICS. I CAN NOW REVEAL THAT EVERY DAY, IN THE USA, OUR RADAR INSTRUMENTS CAPTURE OBJECTS OF FORM AND COMPOSITION UNKNOWN TO US. AND THERE ARE THOUSANDS OF WITNESS REPORTS AND A QUANTITY OF DOCUMENTS TO PROVE THIS, BUT NOBODY WANTS TO MAKE THEM PUBLIC. WHY? BECAUSE THE AUTHORITIES ARE AFRAID THAT PEOPLE MAY THINK OF GOD KNOWS WHAT KIND OF HORRIBLE INVADERS. SO THE PASSWORD STILL IS "WE HAVE TO AVOID PANIC BY ALL MEANS."

Cooper continues:

I WAS, FURTHERMORE, A WITNESS TO AN EXTRAORDINARY PHENOMENON, HERE ON THIS PLANET EARTH. IT HAPPENED IN FLORIDA. THERE I SAW WITH MY OWN EYES A DEFINED AREA OF GROUND BEING CONSUMED BY FLAMES, WITH FOUR INDENTATIONS LEFT BY A FLYING OBJECT WHICH HAD DESCENDED IN THE MIDDLE OF A FIELD. BEINGS HAD LEFT THE CRAFT (THERE WERE OTHER TRACES TO PROVE THIS). THEY SEEMED TO HAVE STUDIED TOPOGRAPHY, THEY HAD

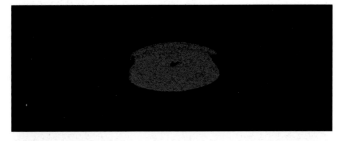

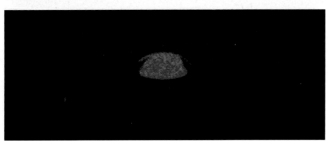

• Here is a selection of NASA space shots that reveal intriguing anomalies. These pictures were provided by ex-NATO intelligence officer Bob Dean.

- NASA's standard response to the Bob Dean pictures is that they are just images of lens flare and other optical illusions that naturally occur in space rather than evidence of extraterrestrial spacecraft. Dean, who has apparently spent large amounts of time and money trying to persuade NASA to release such images, remains adamant that they reveal UFOs monitoring the Earth rather than tricks of the light.

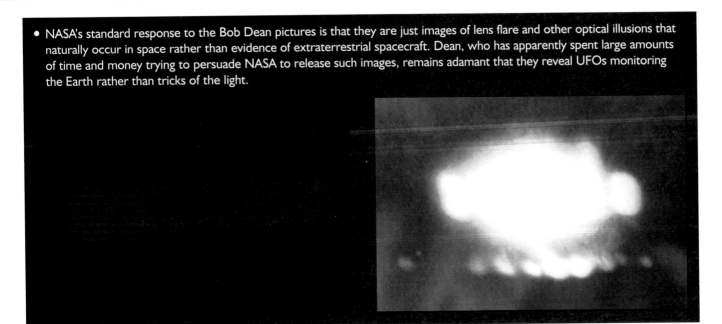

COLLECTED SOIL SAMPLES AND EVENTUALLY, THEY RETURNED TO WHERE THEY HAD COME FROM DISAPPEARING AT ENORMOUS SPEED ... I HAPPEN TO KNOW THAT THE AUTHORITIES DID JUST ABOUT EVERYTHING TO KEEP THIS INCIDENT FROM THE PRESS AND TV, IN FEAR OF A PANICKY REACTION FROM THE PUBLIC.

- Ed White saw a UFO with long protrusions over Hawaii. His photos have never been released.

Other astronauts to make their experience of UFOs public include Ed White, the first American to walk in space, and James McDivitt. In June 1965 the two astronauts, whilst piloting a Gemini spacecraft, were passing over Hawaii when they observed a strange-looking metallic object. The object had long arms sticking out of it. Despite McDivitt taking pictures of the object with a cine-camera, nobody has ever seen these pictures because, it is claimed, the government will not release them.

Some of the most startling evidence given by astronauts comes in the form of taped conversations between the astronauts and ground control staff. The following is an alleged conversation between Neil Armstrong and Edwin 'Buzz' Aldrin shortly after their historic moon landing in Apollo II on 21st July 1969. The conversation was picked up by unnamed radio hams who had bypassed NASA's broadcasting outlets:

NASA: What's there? Mission Control calling Apollo II.
Apollo II: These babies are huge. Sir! Enormous! Oh my God! You wouldn't believe it! I am telling you there are other spacecraft out there. Lined up on the far side of the crater edge! There on the moon watching us!

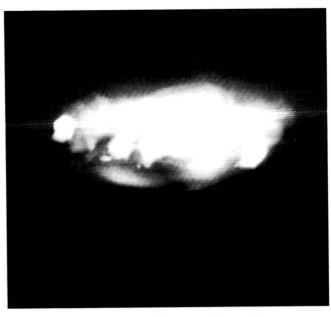

- Neither has NASA been able to provide any adequate explanation for this enormous-looking UFO – none, so far, that it is prepared to release to a general public hungry for more UFO-related information.

After this event, NASA hosted a symposium and a well-respected professor – who wished to remain anonymous – became engaged in a discussion with Armstrong.

Professor: What really happened out there with Apollo II?
Armstrong: It was incredible. Of course we had always known there was a possibility, the fact is we were warned off [by the aliens]. There was never any question then of a space station or a moon city.
Professor: How do you mean "warned off"?
Armstrong: I can't go into details except to say that their ships were far superior to ours both in size and technology. Boy were they big! ... And menacing! There is no question of a space station.
Professor: But NASA had other missions after Apollo II?
Armstrong: Naturally – NASA was committed at that time, and couldn't risk panic on Earth. But it really was a quick scoop and back again.

• Armstrong remains reticent, but he's coming under increasing pressure to put the record straight about just what he saw on the moon ...

Even more amazing was the revelation by Dr Aleksandr Kasantsev that Buzz Aldrin had taken color movie footage of the UFO from inside the space module, and continued filming after he and Armstrong went outside. This film has never been seen, and although Armstrong did confirm that the story was true, he refused to give any further details.

Another astronaut with a tale to tell is Donald Slayton. Slayton, a Mercury astronaut, revealed in an interview that he had seen a UFO while in the air force in 1951.

"I was testing a P-51 fighter in Minneapolis when I spotted this object. I was at about 10,000 feet on a nice, bright, sunny afternoon. I thought the object was a kite, then I realized that no kite is gonna fly that high. As I got closer it looked like a weather balloon, gray and about 3 feet in diameter. But as soon as I got behind the darn thing it didn't look like a balloon anymore. It looked like a saucer, a disk. About the same time I realized that it was suddenly going away from me – and there I was running at

THESE BABIES ARE HUGE. SIR! ENORMOUS! OH MY GOD! YOU WOULDN'T BELIEVE IT! I AM TELLING YOU THERE ARE OTHER SPACECRAFT OUT THERE. LINED UP ON THE FAR SIDE OF THE CRATER EDGE! THERE ON THE MOON WATCHING US!

about 300 miles per hour. I tracked it for a little way, and then all of a sudden the damn thing just took off. It pulled about a 45° climbing turn, accelerated and just flat disappeared."

Moving forward to December 1965, Gemini astronauts James Lovell and Frank Borman also saw a UFO during their second orbit of their record-breaking 14-day flight. Borman reported that he had seen an unidentified spacecraft some distance from their capsule. Gemini Control at Cape Kennedy told

WERE THE MOON-LANDING PHOTOS FAKED?

Everyone accepts that Neil Armstrong was the first man to walk on the moon – don't they? After all, there's that celebrated picture of Armstrong taking his "giant leap for mankind." Not according to a small but vociferous band of conspiracy theorists who assert that the photographs NASA released of the moon landings were blatant fakes. The skeptics' arguments revolve around two anomalies – the lack of moon dust evident in the photos of the landing, and the odd light angles, which suggest the use of artificial lighting, the kind used in a professional photographic studio or even a Hollywood film set. Certainly, when one considers the far from helpful lighting and other environmental conditions, such as temperature, on the moon's surface, the photographs do seem suspiciously sharp and well-lit.

One photo, for example, clearly shows the lunar module's landing pads on the moon's surface. If the moon is as dusty as astronomers say, why is there no debris visible on the pads? Dust would surely have been kicked up by the landing module's retro boosters prior to touch down, yet there is not a speck in sight. Furthermore, the footprints the astronauts left

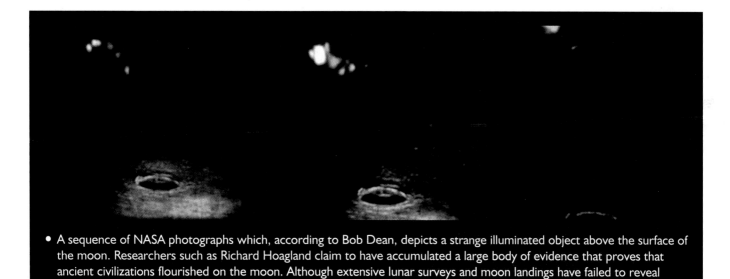

● A sequence of NASA photographs which, according to Bob Dean, depicts a strange illuminated object above the surface of the moon. Researchers such as Richard Hoagland claim to have accumulated a large body of evidence that proves that ancient civilizations flourished on the moon. Although extensive lunar surveys and moon landings have failed to reveal anything, Hoagland is convinced that alien races colonized our lunar neighbor, despite the evidence of frequent lunar probes and lunar landings – assuming, of course, that the moon landings took place (see box below).

him that he was seeing the remains of their own Titan booster rocket, but Borman confirmed that he could see the booster rocket, but that he could also see something completely different.

These are all remarkable stories from astronauts, some confirmed, others maybe myths. It is amusing to speculate, however, whether the pilots of alien craft who encounter Earth spaceships get similarly short shrift when they report the incident to their mission control ...

in the moon's dusty surface seem too well-defined. The footprints captured on film suggest the astronauts had been walking in soft mud rather than deep lunar dust. And then there's the light problem. When another shot of Buzz Aldrin walking on the moon was closely scrutinized, an anomalous light source appeared as a reflection in his visor. The visor shot was blown up to reveal a light hovering above the lunar horizon. Other researchers have studied the angles of lighting in the moon walk photographs and have found them to be inconsistent with the shadows cast by objects on the surface.

Adding an extra twist to this highly controversial conspiracy theory is the allegation that Armstrong told Mission Control the astronauts were being watched by unknown craft of enormous size – could it be that the genuine moonwalk shots were discarded because they revealed UFOs and replaced with the doctored studio shots that were reproduced all over the world's media?

There has been speculation that those responsible for manufacturing the moon-landing shots built in certain tell-tale signs to help future photographic analysts 'decode' the images as fakes. This view is championed by David Percy, professional photographer and Associate of the Royal Photographic Society of the UK, who wrote a convincing article on the subject for the British-based paranormal magazine *Fortean Times*.

● The moon landing shots have become such enduring cultural icons of the 20th century that to question their authenticity seems like heresy. Yet they remain suspiciously slick and professional-looking.

UFO – or Secret Jet?

IN AUGUST 1996, THE WAVERIDER, OR LoFlyte, to give it its correct name, was announced to an unsuspecting world. This revolutionary new aircraft – which is able to attain speeds of up to 3,000 miles per hour by surfing on a stream of air – is the joint accomplishment of NASA and the United States Air Force, and although the prototype has only recently been unveiled, speculation amongst Ufologists is rife. Many Ufologists now assume that the Waverider could have been the mysterious craft sighted by thousands of Belgians between 1989 and 1990, but the suggestion does not carry much credence. First, the Waverider is a wholly different shape from the classic triangular-shaped UFO which was captured on camera during the epidemic of sightings in Belgium. Second, why would the military, in their attempts to keep a secret project from the public – and more importantly, other world military forces – allow it to come to the attention of thousands of skygazers, commercial aircraft and military aircraft?

An equally controversial case is the near-miss involving a British Airways Boeing 737 in 1995. On this occasion the Boeing was returning to Manchester Airport in the UK from Milan, Italy, when it was involved in a near fatal collision with a triangular-shaped object. The pilots, Mark Stuart and Roger Wills, both filed 'Air Near-Miss' reports as a result of their

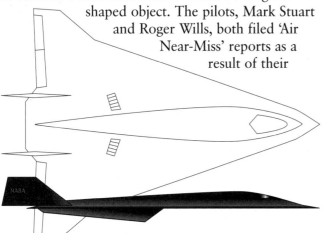

experience, and both claimed that the object passed within feet of their aircraft.

Radar operators were unable to lock on to the object, but observers on the ground did see the object traveling in relation to the Boeing, and confirmed the pilots' report. The pilots drew pictures of the object which they had come into close contact with, and admittedly it did resemble the Waverider, but could it have been? Once again, the answer could only be no. It is quite unthinkable that a US military aircraft would do anything to endanger the lives of innocent civilians for the sake of testing a prototype, but the most convincing reason for the Boeing near-miss not being caused by the Waverider is that the Waverider, as a secret US project, would be required to carry a radar beacon so that air traffic controllers could

- Many Ufologists assume that the Waverider could have been the mysterious craft sighted by thousands of Belgians between 1989 and 1990. Yet it is shaped significantly differently from the triangular-shaped craft that was reported. And why would the military allow so many civilians a sneak glimpse?

BOB DEAN AND "THE ASSESSMENT"

Bob Dean's distinguished war record with the Special Forces in Korea and Vietnam earned him a key job at Supreme Headquarters of Allied Powers Europe (SHAPE) where he claims he discovered the existence of a top secret program he calls "The Assessment." Dean says The Assessment, a comprehensive study of UFO activity around the planet Earth, reveals that mankind has been the subject of an "intensive and massive survey of several extraterrestrial civilizations." The Assessment goes on to say that some kind of process or plan involving aliens is unfolding, but adds that "Military Intelligence analysis has concluded that there did not appear to be a major military threat involved. The conclusions indicate that if [the aliens] were either malevolent or hostile, there was absolutely nothing at that time that we could do."

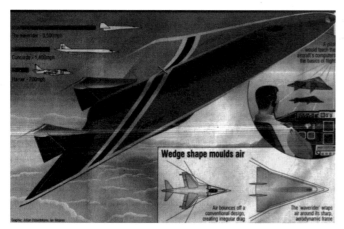

Wedge shape moulds air

© Lockheed Martin Corporation 1996

• The Sea Stealth – a submarine version of the Stealth bomber that can float silently up to an enemy and wreak terrible destruction. Another futuristic weapon based on borrowed alien technology?

identify the craft. This is a prerequisite of carrying out maneuvers in British airspace. So unless the American services are now breaking international regulations we can safely assume that the Manchester near-miss and the Belgian UFO sightings were not the work of the Waverider – and the chances are that we may not know the true culprit for some time yet.

• Two flying saucers zooming through the night sky, or just blips on film? NASA refuses to accept that they may be UFOs, but Dean thinks otherwise.

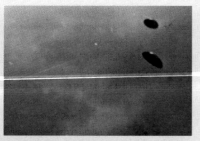

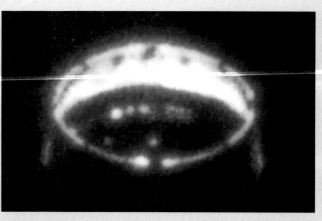

• The shot below left shows a distinctly anomalous looking object hovering over the surface of the moon. The shot below right seems rather less convincing, but Dean is adamant he obtained it from NASA.

• The distinctive cigar-shaped UFO continues to be reported with regularity, particularly in South America and other world hot spots. This appears to be a classic shot.

CHAPTER THREE

CLOSE ENCOUNTERS OF THE THIRD KIND

WITH CLOSE ENCOUNTERS OF THE THIRD KIND, IT STARTS to get personal – this category deals primarily with actually seeing a spaceship and its occupants, either in flight or on the ground. This chapter will also take a look at the overwhelming store of evidence to suggest that UFOs and alien beings do exist.

Physical evidence of a close encounter with extraterrestrials can come in many forms. Rather surprisingly, the most common is the developing of a rash on the body, although some witnesses have reported suffering from ailments akin to radiation sickness, and in some circumstances death can be the end result – as, some Ufologists claim, can be seen in the case of Barney Hill (see Chapter Four). The crop circle enigma is also pointed to as evidence of extraterrestrial spacecraft, these amazing circles being linked to UFOs and their attempts to get their message across to humanity.

The best-documented CE3 is the Roswell incident where an alien spacecraft allegedly crashed in the New Mexico desert. While much of the evidence does indeed indicate a UFO crashed in 1947, skeptics still think otherwise.

Proof of the existence of aliens can be found in many unusual forms and there are none more bizarre than the mysterious "Men in Black," the "enforcers" of cover-up, according to government conspiracy theorists. These strange men appear at the homes of witnesses to UFO activity, often before the witness has even had time to report their sighting. The pattern is generally the same – a garbled conversation with the Men in Black followed by threats to the witness in an attempt to prevent their account becoming public knowledge. The concept of the Men in Black has made a huge impression on authors and film directors, Men in Black-inspired characters appearing in both *The X Files* and *Dark Skies*.

Cattle mutilations are also regarded as having a close link to UFOs, although many observers have claimed that Satanists are the real culprits. How and why such disturbed people would carve up cattle with such surgical precision (as well as leave no signs of struggle) is not explained.

The chapter begins, however, with a look at historical accounts that may have a connection to UFOs – written statements of possible ET activity which in some cases have been overlooked for centuries.

ALIEN AVENGERS AND ANCIENT TECHNOLOGY

AND WHEN THE MORNING AROSE, THEN THE ANGELS HASTENED LOT, SAYING, ARISE, TAKE THY WIFE AND THY TWO DAUGHTERS WHICH ARE HERE, LEST THOU BE CONSUMED IN THE INIQUITY OF THE CITY.

A GOOD PLACE TO START WHEN LOOKING at historical evidence is in the Old Testament, and more specifically at Sodom and Gomorrah. The story of these cities' destruction bears a striking resemblance to modern warfare. In the Book of Genesis, Lot is warned of the immiment disaster:

There follows an eye-witness account of the aftermath of the destruction of Sodom and Gomorrah. Could the cities have been destroyed by a nuclear device, apparently levied against them by an alien race with extremely advanced technology?

The angels tell Lot to take refuge in the mountains, which would make sense if they wished someone not to be harmed by the fallout from a nuclear attack. Rocks are excellent for absorbing radiation, hence the angels' insistence that Lot should head for the mountains and not the plains.

Of course, they could not protect Lot's wife, who turned to look at the destruction of Sodom and Gomorrah and was turned into a pillar of salt. If a nuclear detonation had taken place, she would have been hit by a blast of hot air with a high level of carbon dioxide from the firestorm. This could have triggered runaway chemical reactions in her body, where all the calcium was combined with carbon dioxide, instantly crystallizing her into a block of calcite.

SPARK OF KNOWLEDGE

More concrete proof of alien contact with our ancestors comes in the shape of ancient technology: artefacts which may have been left behind by a departing race. Alternatively, our ancestors could have been taught the methods of fashioning them by alien visitors.

Consider the Baghdad Battery. This "battery" appears to be nothing more than a clay pot, just under 6 inches tall. It is blocked with bitumen, in which is mounted a copper cylinder that runs down about 4 inches inside the pot. Pieces of copper soldered together form the cylinder, which has an iron rod inside it which shows the appearance of having been corroded by acid. The pot dates from between 250BC and 224AD, and was probably in existence during the Parthian domination of Iraq.

• More than just another ancient pot, the Baghdad Battery was a basic battery, complete with acid, which was used to generate electricity as far back as 250BC, archaeologist Wilhelm Konig claimed in 1937. For the Parthians to have made such a huge technological breakthrough implies, some Ufologists claim, extraterrestrial help.

SINCE NO OTHER SOCIETY AT THAT TIME HAD ANY CONCEPT OF HOW TO GENERATE ELECTRICITY, SUCH AN ASTOUNDING BREAKTHROUGH WOULD SUGGEST SOME EXTRATERRESTRIAL ASSISTANCE

The battery was housed at a museum in Iraq until it was discovered by archaeologist Wilhelm Konig in 1937. He instantly saw how this small object could have been used to generate power. Since no other society at that time had any concept of how to generate electricity, such an astounding breakthrough would suggest some extraterrestrial assistance.

Another more astounding find was made in 1900. Sponge divers found the wreck of a ship, which turned out to be over 2000 years old. The find was made off the Greek island of Antikythera. The divers discovered the ship to be stocked to the brim with marble statues and bronze, probably bound for Rome. Amongst the statues a mass of wood and bronze was found. This mass was so badly corroded by the sea water that only a few details could be made out, yet it was apparent that the mass showed the remains of gearwheels and engraved scales. However, the device remained unexplained until 1954, when Derek J. de Solla Price of Cambridge University in the UK, was able to tell the world of its likely use.

He deduced that the mass of wood and bronze was in fact an ancient analog computing device, well ahead of its time. The device was a working model of the stars and planets that could be viewed by the naked eye. Even their relative positions in the sky were shown with stunning accuracy, with pointers indicating the time of day.

No matter what explanations can be given for these apparently advanced devices, there is no mistaking the facts that a humanoid of sorts was alive possibly millions of years before our earliest estimations. This is backed up by a find made in volcanic ash, in Tanzania, East Africa, namely fossilized footprints. The volcanic ash is believed to be 3.6 million years old, and after careful examination it was confirmed that the mysterious footprints were indeed made by a humanoid figure.

- These fossilized footprints were found in 3.6 million-year-old volcanic ash in Tanzania, East Africa. Several anthropologists took measurements of the footprints, and conceded that they were definitely footprints of humanoids rather than coincidental impressions. Since researchers doubt homo erectus existed so long ago, who else could have made the impressions?

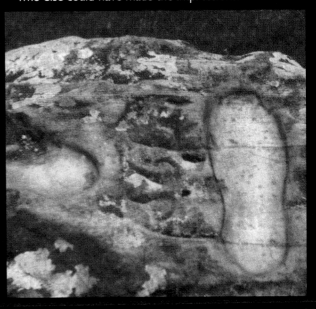

- An artist's impression of the model airplane that was found in an Aztec tomb. Author Erich von Däniken believes such artefacts provide conclusive proof that our ancestors were in close contact with extraterrestrials. Recently, von Däniken has gone so far as to claim that the entire human race has been genetically manipulated by aliens.

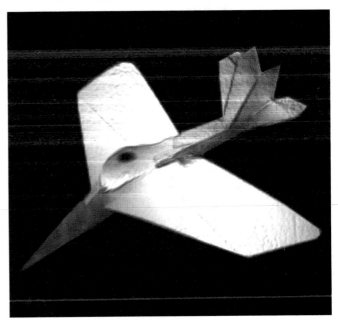

GRISLY GOATSUCKERS

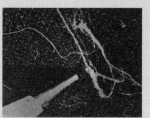

SINCE 1995, THERE HAVE BEEN SOME truly outrageous stories concerning close encounters with alien beings. Consider the Chupacabras, or Goatsucker, as it is more commonly known. This creature has reached legendary status and is feared across the small island of Puerto Rico, where news of it first originated.

The Goatsucker is described as being 3 to 5 feet tall, with huge red eyes, spinal fins, a long appendage that folds inside its mouth, fangs, three long claws and bat-like wings. This grotesque creature, widely believed to be an alien, is responsible for attacking animals on the island and quite literally sucking the blood, and in some cases, the internal organs, from its prey. Even some local islanders have reported being attacked by this creature, although none of these assaults have resulted in fatalities.

It seems that attacks of this kind have been occurring since 1991, although the media did not discover the phenomenon until 1996. Attacks have taken place in Ponce, Aericibo, Dorado and right down to the El Yunque rainforest. Originally the creature was known as *El Vampira Moca*, later to be known as *El Chupacabras*, and its activities are on the increase.

The attacks themselves exhibit a pattern – large amounts of blood are lost from the victim, together with the removal of internal organs. In some circumstances, however, the victim appears to have died as the result of an unknown disease. Many expeditions have been mounted in an attempt to find conclusive evidence for the existence of the Chupacabras, and it is a widely held belief that the creature probably inhabits the many caves which Puerto Rico is famous for. In fact Puerto Rico has such an extensive system of caverns that it was once believed that you could travel via the cave structures to many distant parts of the world.

One such an expedition, led by US researcher Bob Schott, has recovered some curious facts. At the ranch of one Melvin Reyes in Canovanas, the expedition learnt that in April 1996, two of his sheep were attacked. The team heard that one of the sheep was killed by the predator, whilst the other barely survived the attack. Although its tail was torn from the root, the sheep was saved by a constant diet of vitamins.

The team also met up with a local Puerto Rican researcher, Jorge Martin, who accompanied them to the small village of Dorado, where they interviewed witnesses who claimed to have seen a group of Chupacabras in woods behind their homes. On inspection of the woods, strange indentations in the grass were found in the exact location described by the residents. The residents also stated that the Chupacabras were heading towards a weird hovering light.

In October 1996, in Campo Rico, Jorge Martin obtained blood samples recovered from a fence where a Chupacabras allegedly clambered over, only to snag itself before escaping. Another report claims that prior to that event a local policeman had in fact shot at one of the creatures, resulting in the trail of

IS IT ANGEL HAIR OR JUST COBWEBS?

One of the most bizarre arguments for the existence of extraterrestrial intelligence is a substance known as Angel Hair. Angel Hair is very rarely reported but when it is the tales are quite extraordinary. One such incident was published in the **Marine Observer** in October 1963. The ship Roxburgh Castle was moored to her berth in Montreal, Canada, on 10th October 1962. Captain R.H. Pape was taking the air on deck when he noticed "fine white filaments of unknown kind" draped around the railings and stanchions.

"Calling the attention of the Chief Officer, I pulled one of these strands from a stanchion and found it to be quite tough and resilient. I stretched it but it would not break easily (as for instance, a cobweb would have done) and after keeping it in my hand for three or four minutes it disappeared completely: in other words it just vanished into nothing. Looking up we could blood. The results of the blood analysis were remarkable, to say the least.

Apparently the sample exhibited similar characteristics to human blood, but the genetic analysis showed that the blood was in no way compatible with human blood nor any animal known to science.

WHERE COULD IT COME FROM?

As is the case with all outbreaks of panic and conjecture, there are as many theories and rumors as there are half truths. The same can be said for the Chupacabras. One theory is that the creatures are the remnants of an alien race abandoned on this planet after their spacecraft crashed. They have managed to adapt and are now making themselves known to humanity. Why such a technologically advanced race would try to make contact by killing and mutilating livestock has not been adequately explained.

Another theory is that the creatures are actually part of mankind's attempts to clone or hybridize creatures, in an attempt to manufacture the perfect entity. Within this possibility there are many other equally valid points. Why would mankind wish to create such a creature? What purpose could be served by such an animal? There are, of course, some facts to back up these claims. Firstly, Puerto Rico has

been party to hundreds of UFO sightings over the years, and is not that far from Florida, currently a UFO hot spot. Also it is worth considering the rumor that the El Yunque rainforest is not only home to many caves and wildlife, but also to a secret government installation, believed to be a research facility.

The date of the first sightings of the Chupacabras is also significant as it ties in with the hybrid creature theory. In 1989, Hurricane Hugo decimated a large portion of the El Yunque rainforest, and it is thought by some researchers that this disaster allowed the creatures at the research facility to escape into the jungle and caves, where they've dwelled ever since.

The truth is, as always, that the Chupacabras will remain a mystery until one is finally caught – and that may be quite a while yet.

- Chupacabras expert Bob Schott notes there have been numerous UFO sightings in Puerto Rico, and believes the island plays host to a top secret Area 51-style research facility, deep in the rainforest.

- Strange filaments continue to appear around the world at regular intervals. Spiders webs or UFO residue?

see small cocoons of the material floating down from the sky but as far as we could ascertain there was nothing either above or at street level to account for this extraordinary occurrence."

This is a typical account of this remarkable substance, which rapidly dissolves into nothing (this being one of the reasons for the material very rarely being photographed...).

Probably one of the best-documented cases of Angel Hair took place in Oloron-Sainte-Marie, France, on 17th October 1952. A local headmaster was watching a cloud out of his dining room window when he noticed a cylinder-shaped object above the cloud. The object was white in color and tilted at an angle of 45°. The headmaster noticed that white smoke seemed to be detaching itself from the object, and he also observed at least 20 smaller objects traveling in the same direction as the larger

cylinder. These smaller objects were round and made up of the white smoky substance. The headmaster grabbed his binoculars and noticed that each small object was encircled by a yellow ring with a red circle within. All of a sudden he noticed that the smaller spheres were leaving a trail of a threadlike substance which was slowly floating to the ground. Soon the streets, trees and walls were adorned by this strange material.

The locals nicknamed the substance "Threads of the Virgin" and when the substance was touched it became gelatinous and quickly dissolved. This incident baffled the scientific world, whose only explanation was that the threads were little cobwebs left behind by migrating spiders. This theory does not explain why the substance disappeared when handled, however.

A similar occurrence is said to have taken place near Weymouth, in the UK, in the late 1980s. Once again the substance was likened to tiny cobwebs, and vanished when handled. The official explanation for that incident was that the fine strands were detergent residue from a tanker at sea clearing out its bilge pumps, yet once again this theory was brushed aside by the locals who experienced the phenomenon.

Modern Day CE3s – Those Mysterious Men in Black

MEN IN BLACK, OR MIB, HAVE MADE SOME outlandish claims in an attempt to glean information from possible witnesses of UFO sightings. They usually claim to be working for the FBI, CIA, NASA or other governmental establishments, but when their credentials are checked, all too often after a visit and by then too late, they are found to be impostors.

One of the most harrowing MIB visits to date was experienced in 1953 by Albert Bender, Director of the International Flying Saucer Bureau, then based in Connecticut, USA.

Bender had intended to publish his findings on the subject of UFOs and their origin, feeling that he had at last discovered the secret behind flying saucers. Prior to announcing his startling news to the world, Bender felt he should test out his theories on a colleague.

He mailed his detailed dossier to this colleague and within a few days the mysterious MIB arrived at his home. Three sinister visitors dressed all in black appeared in Bender's bedroom, where he had been lying after experiencing a dizzy spell. He at first noticed the figures as a shadowy appearance, but they soon began to take on a clearer form. Bender noticed that they all dressed identically in black suits and wore Homburg hats (a felt hat with narrow

- Albert Bender holding up a diagram of one of the many anomalous craft he encountered, prior to his visit from the Men in Black.

curled brim and a dent in the crown).

"The men all looked at me," explained Bender, "their eyes suddenly lighting up like flashlight bulbs. They were burning into my very soul, and the pain above my eyes became unbearable. It was then that I sensed that they were conveying a message to me by telepathy."

One of the men was holding a copy of Bender's journal, and they confirmed to him that his theories about UFOs were correct. The strangers even offered additional information. Bender was so terrified by this visitation that when the MIB demanded that he close down his organization and forget about publishing his findings, he complied without hesitation.

Bender did, however, mention this encounter to fellow colleagues within the UFO fraternity. One of these was Gray Barker, who later went on to publish a highly controversial book, *They Knew Too Much About Flying Saucers*. Bender himself eventually published a book entitled *Flying Saucers And The Three Men*, as a rebuke to his friends who had been demanding an explanation for his amusing visitation. What they got was a story more remarkable than any science fiction tale. Bender's book included detailed accounts of Earth's interaction with extraterrestrials and the founding of an alien base in Antarctica. It is now felt that this literary effort was designed by Bender as a red herring for his colleagues, and that he never disclosed the real truth about UFOs – hence keeping his word to the MIB.

VISITORS FROM SPACE

This was not to be Gray Barker's only involvement with the Men in Black. He was to come up against them once again when investigating strange sightings of UFOs with John Keel, investigations which were later published in *Visitors From Space*. On this occasion, it involved a small West Virginian town called Mount Pleasant.

According to *Visitors From Space*, the local reporter for the *Mount Pleasant Messenger*, Mary Hyre, was the first to receive a visit from the MIB. Mary was sitting in her office sifting through records of known deaths following the collapse of the town's 700-foot Silver Bridge, when two strangers entered the room. She had been inundated with visitors all week, including relatives of the bridge victims and tired rescue workers, so when her door opened once more she barely looked up from her desk.

However, when Mary looked up, she was greeted with the most peculiar sight. Two men stood before her. They appeared to be almost like twins, and both were short and dressed in black overcoats. She later

THE JEAN-PIERRE PRÉVOST INCIDENT

December 1979 saw one of the most sensational MIB encounters ever reported. It involved the alleged alien abduction of Frenchman Franck Fontaine in the French town of Cengy-Pontoise. What was of particular importance about this case was the length of time that Fontaine was missing (apparently seven days) and the ensuing threats made to him, Jean-Pierre Prévost and Salomon N'Diaye by three mysterious men in black.

According to Prévost, on the eve of Friday 7th December, the three men had sat up almost all night talking, before eventually retiring to bed at around 5:30 am. However, their rest was short-lived as at 7 am Prévost heard the doorbell ring, and got up to answer the door. He was faced with three men. One was of medium build wearing a dark green suit – so dark it was almost black. He had a short beard and well kept black hair. The other two were much stockier in build by comparison.

The following description is the most startling aspect of the encounter because Prévost was certain that the three visitors did not exist in the conventional sense. He stated that the three visitors had no sight – instead their eyes were a fixed white mass which was quite terrifying. The bearded man asked Prévost if he was one of the three, meaning one of the UFO witnesses, to which the Frenchman answered yes. The man went on to say that Prévost must pass a message on to his other two friends.

The message was that they had already said too much and if they continued to talk of the events surrounding the abduction they would have an "accident." Furthermore, if they still insisted on speaking of these events, an even worse fate would befall them. With this, the three strangers simply vanished. Prévost was to see these three men on several occasions after this incident but only one more threat was made, and this was once again a warning to stop talking about their experiences. He later described these visitors as being "intra-terrestrial," in other words people who came from within the Earth as opposed to outer space, hence their ability to travel through dimensions and vanish without a trace.

recalled that their complexions were dark, and almost oriental in nature. The two then spoke: "We hear there has been a lot of UFO activity around here." Mary was astounded, as the bridge had been the main topic of conversation in Mount Pleasant and UFOs could not have been further from her mind. However, she answered their questions with a yes, as the area had seen its fair share of UFO activity. She handed them a huge file of newspaper clippings relating to the numerous sightings in the vicinity. They gave the file a glance and handed it back, almost nonchalantly.

What followed was even more bizarre. The men asked if Mary had ever been told not to publish such stories, and if not, what her reaction would be if she was told to stop writing about flying saucers. "I would say go to hell," was Mary's response. The two men looked at each other, and Mary looked away. When she glanced up again they had vanished.

ANOTHER VISITOR COMES A-CALLING

Mary Hyre had just about recovered from her first visit when the door flew open once again. This time it was another odd-looking character, who appeared even more oriental than the other two. Mary noticed that his hands were particularly weird, with long tapering fingers. The visitor wore a dishevelled black suit, which was slightly out of fashion. Even more bizarre was the fact that he did not bother to wear any sort of overcoat or jacket, despite the freezing conditions outside.

The man introduced himself as Jack Brown, a UFO researcher. Mary was drawn into discussion with "Jack" about the local UFO sightings, and then questioned, just as in her earlier visit, about whether she had any plans to publish the accounts.

Mary immediately demanded to know whether "Jack" was an associate of the other two MIB. The visitor denied any knowledge of the other two, claiming instead that he was a friend of Gray Barker. Barker was a researcher of wide renown at the time, so Mary was reassured when his name was mentioned. However, it appeared that "Jack Brown" did not hold Barker's friend, John Keel, in the same high regard, remarking that Keel was a liar for saying that he had personally witnessed UFOs. The meeting between Mary Hyre and "Jack Brown" came to the same sudden end, as "Jack" seemingly disappeared while Mary

WHAT IS THEIR PURPOSE?

One constant in virtually all the detailed reports of Men in Black is that they appear to be totally incompetent. They pose as military personnel, but dress in the wrong uniform for the department they claim to be representing. When posing as civilians, the strangers appear to be a decade or two behind modern times, both in dress sense and choice of car.

Often the cars are very old models, yet appear to be in pristine condition and when the license plates are checked out, the make and model of car comes up as never having existed.

Surprisingly, MIB have sometimes shown that they are not even familiar with such everyday objects as pens and lighters. On one occasion, an MIB even had to be shown how to hold a knife and fork in order to eat the food offered by his dumbfounded host!

Despite these almost comical traits, the intentions of the MIB are still a frightening and a very real enigma. They often threaten UFO witnesses with menaces and make the witness fully aware of the consequences should they decide to ignore their warning. However, there is no recorded proof that any witness has come

looked away for a moment. It appears that "Jack" visited quite a few UFO witnesses in the area, managing to confuse the witnesses with mindless ramblings whilst stumbling around and behaving in an odd, unnerving manner. It's uncertain whether Gray Barker and "Jack Brown" ever met, or for that matter whether Barker ever came into contact with MIB personally, but it is obvious that these odd characters were well aware of his research.

DR HOPKINS AND THE OTHERWORLDLY VISITOR

One evening in September 1976 in Maine, Dr Herbert Hopkins received a call from a man who claimed to be the Vice President of the New Jersey UFO Research Organization. The man asked if he could meet with Dr Hopkins to discuss a case that Hopkins had been involved with.

Hopkins was alone at the time as his family had gone out for the evening, so he agreed to the request.

Having put down the phone, he went to his back door to switch on the light so that the man could to grief as a result of choosing to disregard these threats.

One of the many theories surrounding the Men in Black is that they are the invention of their victim's psyche. UFO witnesses are sometimes thought to have a heightened psychic ability, which may in turn make them more vulnerable to a visitation. This theory suggests that the appearance of the MIB at a witness's door soon after a sighting may have something to do with a telepathic link between the witness and the stranger, a link which makes the witness an easily traceable target.

Another possible explanation for these odd characters is that they hail from a realm within our own world, but are probably still visitors to this planet. They may be emissaries of a race with a vested interest in Earth, their presence at the homes of witnesses to UFO phenomena being necessary in order to keep their identity and perhaps even their Earth bases a secret.

Within the possibilities of this theory is the plausible chance that MIB may even be automatons or robots, sent to carry out a mission by their keepers. This may well account for some of the odd behavior exhibited, their lack of worldliness, their inability to eat, their need to leave a witness's home because their "power" is running low, and their lack of true emotion.

find his way up the path safely, only to find the man already halfway up the porch stairs. Hopkins later remarked that he saw no car, and that even if the man did have a car, it was impossible for him to have reached his house from a nearby phone in such a short time.

The doctor invited the man in, noticing that he was dressed all in black with a black hat and shoes to match. When the man removed his hat, Hopkins observed that he was bald. He also noticed that the man had no eyelashes or eyebrows. His skin was as white as a corpse and his lips were bright red, as if he was wearing theatrical make-up. During their conversation, Hopkins noticed that the stranger would occasionally rub his mouth with his glove, which left a trail of lipstick on the glove and a smear on the man's mouth.

Hopkins continued with the meeting and pondered on the stranger aspects of the night after the man had left. Hopkins later stated that the man had told him that he had two coins in his pocket and that he would like the doctor to put one of the coins in his hand, which he did. The visitor then told Hopkins that "nobody on this planet will ever see that coin again."

The conversation about UFOs continued for a while longer until the man rose to his feet, rather

unsteadily, and announced that his energy was running low and that he ought to go. He left the house and stumbled down the porch stairs. At this point Hopkins spotted a bright bluish-white light in the driveway, which he first thought to be the man's car, but on reflection the light was unlike any normal car headlight. The case Hopkins was working on at the time involved the possible teleportation of a UFO in Maine. Being a hypnotist, Hopkins had conducted a number of sessions with eye-witnesses of the teleportation. After the man's visit, Hopkins was so disturbed that he willingly agreed to the man's demands, and later that day he erased the tapes of the hypnosis sessions. Later checks confirmed that the so-called New Jersey UFO Research Organization did not exist.

UFO CRASH –
THE ROSWELL AFFAIR

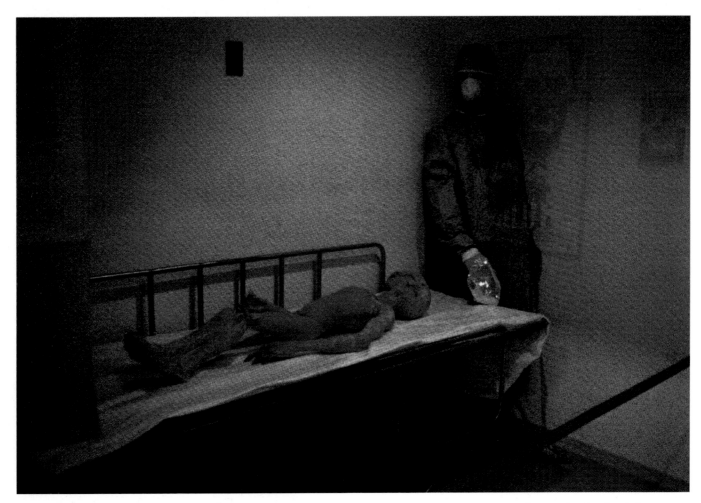

ON 2ND JULY, 1947, AN ALIEN SPACECRAFT crashed on rancher Mac Brazel's farm in Roswell, New Mexico, an incident which spawned one of the greatest UFO mysteries of all time. Fifty years on, it is still not fully resolved, causing the US government to be accused of a cover-up on an enormous scale.

The facts of the case are quite easy to follow. On the night in question, several eye-witnesses reported seeing a brilliant, glowing object hurtling towards the ground; the impact site was guessed at being just outside the small town of Roswell, New Mexico. Later that evening the craft did crash land, and three of the occupants died on impact, however, a fourth was recovered from the scene, only to die later in a military hospital.

Mac Brazel, who originally made the find, later stated that he wished that he had never said anything about the incident in the first place, especially given the subsequent media interest.

It's likely that even the US military now wish they could travel back in time as well, to quell the outrage and disinformation that they managed to create with their initial statement that they had recovered a downed alien spaceship – a statement which they quickly retracted, replacing it with the more mundane claim that what they had recovered was nothing more than a weather balloon. This statement was issued by General Roger Ramay, and the military even went to the extreme measures of having Major Jesse Marcel photographed examining the alleged

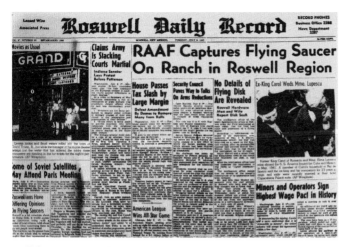

- Fifty years on, the debate about Roswell still rages. Ironically, it was the military itself which first announced an alien spaceship had been found, rather than a Ufologist. Faced with a public furore, officials soon retracted their story, claiming that the Roswell craft had in fact turned out to be a weather balloon.

- Major Jesse Marcel

debris from the balloon wreckage. However, none of this managed to dampen the public fervor for the case and stories and rumors abounded. A local nurse came forward to claim that she had been asked to sit in on an autopsy of two of the aliens recovered, and an undertaker stated that he had received a call from the military, asking for a number of small coffins. Even more bizarre were the claims from locals who said that they had made it out to Brazel's ranch before the military had arrived and had seen with their own eyes the dead bodies, which were later recovered by the military. They described

THREE OF THE OCCUPANTS DIED ON IMPACT, HOWEVER, A FOURTH WAS RECOVERED FROM THE SCENE, ONLY TO DIE LATER IN A MILITARY HOSPITAL

the beings as very small, with spindly bodies. The beings were apparently in an advanced state of decay, due to night predators and the length of time that they had been exposed to the elements. The interest in the case never died down and eminent researchers from all four corners of the globe arrived at their

THE RONALD JOHNSON SIGHTING

On the evening of 2nd November 1971, farmer's son Ronald Johnson, of Delphos near Kansas, was in for the surprise of his life.

Johnson was tending sheep on his father's farm when he noticed a mushroom-shaped object, covered in multicolored lights, hovering just 2 feet from the ground. The object was only 25 yards from Johnson, who was able to get a good look at the craft's details and estimated that the object was about 10 feet in diameter. Johnson watched in awe for a moment before the object shot off issuing a bright light from its underside, which temporarily blinded him. After recovering from the initial shock Johnson rushed into his house and summoned his family, who all raced outside in time to see the object, now high in the sky, vanish over the horizon. However, the story does not end there. On inspection of the area where the object had hovered, the family were stunned to notice a glowing ring on the ground and a luminescence on parts of the trees surrounding the area. Johnson's mother, a nurse, touched the surrounding soil and later reported that it made her fingers go numb, almost as if a local anesthetic had been administered. This condition lasted for a very worrying two weeks before it eased.

A week later it snowed and the snow settled everywhere, except on the ring. Further examination of the ring and the soil showed that the ground directly beneath it was impermeable to water and that the soil contained a large quantity of an organism known as Nocardia, which can often be found growing alongside a fungus (which at times can appear to be fluorescent). It was believed that energy from the UFO had triggered the ring's growth. Johnson also suffered headaches, eye infections and recurring nightmares as a result of his encounter.

- The tiny New Mexican town of Roswell has certainly benefited from the UFO tourist industry spawned by the crash. The Roswell museum (above) is an excellent resource for anyone seeking historical information on the event, but the military stands by its story – if bodies of dead aliens were recovered from the craft, no-one is letting on.

own conclusions, and many investigations into the real facts of the incident were launched. Campaigners have constantly striven to have the official documentation on the Roswell incident released under the Freedom of Information Act, but no relevant or useful information has ever been forthcoming.

- If a UFO did crash, what happened to the bodies of the occupants? Are they still being held by the military authorities? This model alien, taken from the movie *Roswell,* would suggest that the corpses emerged relatively unscathed. It's more likely that they would have been quite badly mangled by the impact, however, or mutilated by animals.

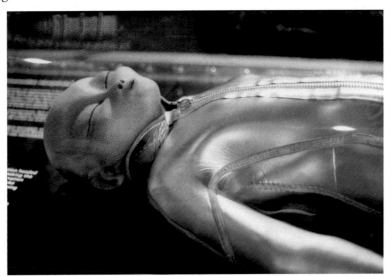

THE VARGHINA UFO CRASH

Several Central American Ufologists believe that a UFO may have crashed in a remote part of Varghina, Brazil, on 20th January 1996. Three girls were coming down a narrow path in an area known as Jardim Andere, close to the city center, when one of the girls recoiled in terror. She'd seen a creature with slippery brownish skin and what appeared to be three small horns protruding from its head. The eyes were described as huge and red, and the creature was seen to be squatting down with its long arms dangling between its legs. The creature was observed for a few minutes, until it made a sudden movement which prompted the girls to run away in terror.

Earlier on the same day, a UFO was reported by two farmhands who also lived locally. They claimed to have seen a huge grey object the size of a small bus. The object was also likened to a floating submarine with white smoke trailing from the back of the object as it gently glided just above the ground.

The case soon received world-wide attention and even Harvard professor and abduction researcher John Mack made a visit to the region. It wasn't long before more and more details

ROSWELL ON THE SLAB

In 1995, British businessman Ray Santilli dropped a bombshell on the UFO community with his claims that he had purchased, for an undisclosed sum, a film depicting the original footage of an autopsy allegedly carried out on two of the dead beings recovered from the Roswell wreckage. This revelation sparked a storm of controversy and many Ufologists claimed that the film was nothing more than an elaborate scam. After showing the footage at a BUFORA (British UFO Research Association) conference in August of that year, special effects experts began were disclosed. Posters were erected in the town asking for witnesses to come forward, and the information gleaned was unbelievable.

It was reported that the alien spacecraft crashed and up to seven occupants were captured. Eye-witnesses claimed that one of these was dead, and one was injured and the other five, after hiding in the nearby towns of Varghina and Jardim Andere, were eventually flushed out and captured by the authorities.

Rumors of US involvement in the possible retrieval of a spacecraft were also rife. According to a Brazilian UFO magazine, a US civilian was present when the wreckage of a presumed cigar-shaped UFO was loaded aboard a flatbed truck on the morning of 20th January 1996.

The case is still under constant investigation and it's even been dubbed the Roswell of the 1990s. Most mysterious of all, the descriptions of the Brazilian aliens almost mirror those of the Chupacabras in Puerto Rico; if they were found to be the same creature it is possible to conclude that they do come from another planet, as opposed to a government laboratory.

Some of the best evidence for the existence of aliens, is also sadly, often the most bizarre. More often than not these stories are frowned upon and considered to be the invention of an overactive mind, but in some cases not even the human mind could conjure up such remarkable stories and staggering descriptions of beings which have been encountered.

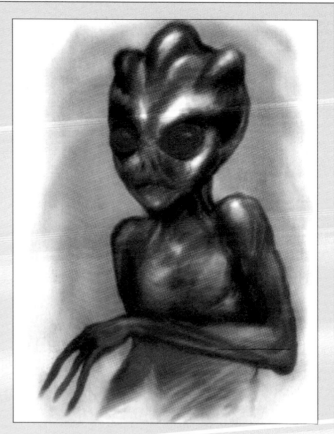

● Artist's impression of the Varghina alien.

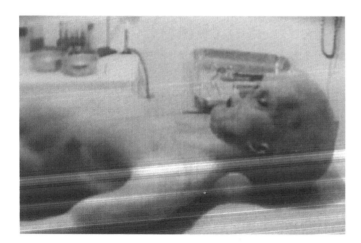

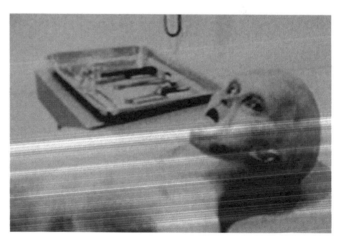

● These stills were taken from a video of the Roswell crash autopsy that Ray Santilli claims to have obtained from the cameraman present at the original examination. Despite the

authentically terrifying-looking alien, there are some inconsistencies: a phone that can be seen on one of the walls for example, is suspiciously modern for 1947.

to come forward claiming that the whole film could easily be recreated, and that the film was nothing more than a hoax. This did not, however, prevent a curious public from buying the official video in droves. Possibly the most worrying aspects of the

footage are that the creatures shown in the film bear no resemblance to the beings described in 1947 by eye-witnesses, in as much as they appeared much too tall to have been the aliens killed in the Roswell crash. The creatures in the video seem very human in

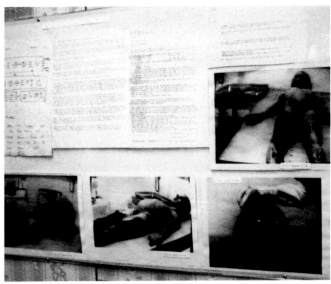

appearance, heightening speculation that the bodies were those of people who had either died as a result of germ warfare, or an equally unpleasant disease called Talbots Syndrome. Finally, the cameraman apparently said the footage dates from June 1947, one month *before* the crash took place. Could this be an autopsy of a corpse from an earlier UFO crash?

The public demanded information from Santilli, wanting to know the results of tests carried out on the film stock, the identity of the cameraman and why the film had taken so long to surface. A few

IN TIME THE CREATURE PRODUCED A CRYSTAL FROM ITS CHEST WHICH SHOWED THE WHOLE OF MANKIND'S HISTORY AND THE GALAXY IN A STRANGE FORM OF HOLOGRAPHICS

answers were forthcoming: the film stock may have come from 1947, but this is no guarantee that this is when the footage was shot with the film – it could have been simply stored for several decades before being used. The cameraman's identity has never been

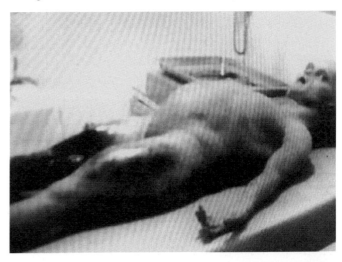

1890

CORNWALL, ENGLAND
EARLY ENGLISH SIGHTING
One of the earliest recorded sightings of occupants of an alien spacecraft occurred in 1890 in Cornwall, south-west England. Two farmhands reported seeing what sounded like a spacecraft with small dwarf-like beings at the controls. A subsequent investigation failed to reveal any further anomalies.

1896/7

AURORA, TEXAS
FORERUNNER OF ROSWELL?
On 17th April 1897, numerous eyewitnesses claimed that an airship crashed into a windmill in Aurora, Texas, a town which no longer exists. The occupant of the ship, who didn't survive the impact, was described as non-human and the corpse was duly buried in the town's cemetery.

1947

NEAR BAURU, BRAZIL
DISTURBING ENTITIES
José Higgins was working on a survey crew when he encountered three entities. He described them as 7 feet tall, wearing "transparent suits covering head and body, and inflated like rubber bags." They were carrying metal boxes. Higgins was the only real witness as the rest of his colleagues fled in horror.

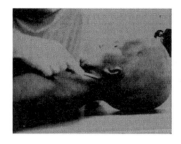

• Several special effects experts reckon a Roswell-style alien could be created fairly easily. Other skeptics have suggested this was a human corpse, disfigured by disease or warfare.

revealed; although speculation was rife that he would make a statement in the form of an interview in 1996. The reason why the footage has taken so long to make its way into the public's hands is fairly mundane. Apparently the cameraman found himself in need of money and decided to cash in on the film's notoriety. Yet this doesn't explain how it was possible for a military cameraman to smuggle out a copy of such a highly classified subject from under the noses of the very people wishing to cover up the incident? Why does the cameraman not speak for himself – after all he must have known that he would be in public demand, surely he was prepared for this? And finally, *when* will Santilli reveal the ultimate proof of the video's authenticity?

The Terra Papers

At the height of interest in the Roswell video, Native American mystic Robert Morning Sky claimed that in the same year as the infamous Roswell crash, a second saucer came down in the same vicinity as the first – only this time Robert's grandfather and five other men managed to get to the object before the military arrived. Furthermore, they managed to recover one of the beings, alive. The six men nursed the being back to health and eventually formed a bond with the so-called "Star Elder." In time the creature

• Did President Truman also make an appearance in the Roswell video? Truman was fully briefed about the 1947 crash, and some conspiracy theorists even claim he appeared on the video in a section which was later cut. The owner of the Roswell video, Ray Santilli, has confirmed Truman appears, but the clip has never been made public.

produced a crystal from its chest which showed the whole of mankind's history and the galaxy in a strange form of holographics. The alien informed the six Native Americans of a war raging in space between differing species, and that humans were a genetically engineered life form under constant scrutiny by the beings who created them. All these and other revelations were published in a book by Morning Sky, called *The Terra Papers*. Morning Sky is adamant that two UFOs crashed in July 1947, and that his writings are proof that his grandfather not only witnessed the second event, but even managed to intervene.

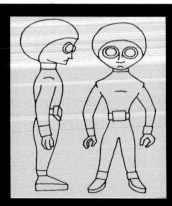

1954
Shrewsbury, England
Aliens in "Ski Suits"
Jennie Roestenberg and her children observed a UFO hovering above their house on 11th October. Two beings were seen through transparent panels in the side of the craft, wearing turquoise blue outfits which resembled ski suits. Mrs Roestenberg later sketched the aliens (left).

1954
Quaroubles, France
Armless Entities
In September Marius Dewilde met a pair of 3 feet-tall beings without arms, shuffling along on short legs. He went on to report seeing a "shape" nearby, from which shot a white green light that paralyzed him before flying off. An engineer examined the ground marks, and claimed only a 30-ton weight could have made them.

1954
Caracas, Venezuela
Hairy Dwarf Attack
Two truck drivers saw a shining object hovering about 6 feet off the ground on 28th November. When they investigated, one of them was attacked by a creature described as a hairy dwarf-like animal with glowing eyes. Their story was verified by a local doctor who claimed to have witnessed the whole incident.

SALVAGING THE TRUTH

COULD THIS BLURRY PHOTO BE A GENUINE picture of the ship that supposedly crashed outside Roswell, New Mexico, in July 1947?

The British UFO magazine *Alien Encounters* was sent this picture by a reader who also provided some details about the origin of the alleged UFO crash site photo. The original of the picture is in the possession of an ex-serviceman, who wishes to remain anonymous for the moment, going only by the initials DS. DS, who lives in Houston, Texas, claims that he was given the picture in 1953 by a senior

officer while he was based at Fort Worth Army Air Force Base. DS says he was led to believe that the photo had been confiscated from a civilian eye-witness. After receiving the photo, DS kept it a carefully guarded family secret, which was only discussed infrequently due to its sensitive nature. Why DS's superior officer gave him the picture is unknown, but DS now wants it to receive wider exposure. DS himself believes that the ship is some kind of probe, but has seen no corroborating documentation to confirm this.

Is the picture genuine, or is it, as so many UFO pictures have proven to be in the past, a fake? Under scrutiny, a case can be made for both arguments. The official line on the Roswell incident today is that the "saucer" was actually a downed observation device codenamed Project Mogul. Mogul's purpose was to

THE GENUINE ARTICLE?

Is the picture of a crashed UFO real or fake? This at-a-glance guide was compiled after seeking the advice of a team of photographic experts. Examine the facts, and make up your own mind ...

REAL

TERRAIN
The rocky, sparsely vegetated ground is consistent with eye-witness accounts of the Roswell crash site.

LIGHTING
The harsh lighting, with clearly defined shadows and glaring highlights, is what one would expect to find in midsummer in New Mexico. If the picture was of a small model, this kind of lighting would be hard to simulate.

SHAPE
Even though the *Roswell Daily Record* reported a "flying disk," in keeping with the flying saucer mania that had just struck the nation, the object here appears more ovoid in form, with a truncated rear. Again, this is consistent with some of the eye-witness accounts. There are no existing models of this shape, so it would have had to be built from scratch – a difficult job, considering the object's smooth compound curves.

SIZE
Most of the eye-witness accounts of the crash site place the size of the ship at around 50 feet in length. As the soldiers appear to be at the top of a small rise that leads down a short way to the ship itself, the size of the vessel seems to be on a par with accounts.

SCALE
There is still a sense of scale in this blurred image – the soldiers and ship in the foreground have more intense shadows and highlights than the background. This reduction of contrast over distance is hard to reproduce on a model.

be sent aloft by balloon to monitor the Soviet Union's nuclear tests, hence the secrecy and the cover-up. However, this explanation ignores the numerous eye-witness accounts of debris that bore no resemblance to any known material, and also Jesse Marcel's statements that the wreckage he found was unlike anything that the air force operated.

"One thing I was certain of, being familiar with all our activities, was that it was not a weather balloon, nor an aircraft, nor a missile. It was something else." Marcel was the base's intelligence officer, so would be fully briefed, even about secret projects.

There is even a theory that the UFO didn't crash near Roswell at all, but at Socorro, New Mexico. In 1950, a civil engineer called Grady Barnett revealed that he had come across a crashed UFO, with small, humanoid bodies around the wreckage, at Magdelena, near Socorro, New Mexico. Barnett went on to report seeing a group of archeologists in the vicinity, examining the aliens. Shortly afterwards, a military unit arrived on the scene and made all the

witnesses swear an oath of silence. Barnett's story was picked up by Ufologists who went on to claim that the main Roswell UFO ran into trouble near Roswell but didn't actually crash until it reached San Augustin. The alien bodies were retrieved by the military and kept at the Wright Patterson Air Force Base. There are also stories from 1947 that the recovered "flying disk" had actually collided with another UFO, as one witness claims to have seen a badly damaged ship with a large indentation in its hull, as if something had flown into it. This could link in with unconfirmed reports that the cameraman who filmed the Roswell autopsy said he filmed the event in June 1947, one month before the Roswell crash. Could there have been two separate crashes?

Again, the details of these stories are too patchy to be conclusive. Obviously, not every UFO crash story can be genuine, because if this were the case the countryside would be littered with downed spacecraft, but the facts strongly suggest that something odd crashed in New Mexico in 1947.

FAKE

FOCUS

Even though the picture sent to ALIEN ENCOUNTERS was a duplicate of the original, and therefore some blurriness was to be expected, the fact that *everything* in the photo is out of focus is suspicious. Defocusing an image to hide flaws is a renowned photographic trick.

SHIP

Although the ship is lying at an angle that suggests it skidding to a stop against a rise, there is no visible sign of damage. Accounts from the site would lead one to expect more crash damage to the ship's hull – one witness claimed that one side of the ship had been ripped open.

"FAT ARM"

The right-hand soldier's left arm appears to be extremely bulky. This might suggest the use of toy figures.

SOLDIERS

The figures on the left and right (presumably soldiers investigating the crash) appear to be standing in an identical pose. Again, it is possible that they are toy soldiers standing in a model diorama.

PHOTO

The owner of the photo refuses to release the original picture for analysis. Without authentication of the photo's age, the image has to be regarded with skepticism.

THOSE WEIRD AND WONDERFUL SPACEMEN

HIDDEN IN THE ANNALS OF UFOLOGY ARE some chronicles of encounters with the most extraordinary creatures. The following is a small representation of the most bizarre meetings with beings from other worlds.

- A driver in Argentina apparently saw these distinctly sinister beings walking along a road in 1971. They were heading directly towards him and their eyes were giving off a strange light. By the time he reached the group they had disappeared. Like many Close Encounters of the Second Kind, all we have is an artist's impression.

THE FLATWOODS FIEND

On 12th September 1952, in Flatwoods, West Virginia, a group of young children saw what they thought was a meteor land on a nearby hillside. The children accompanied by a neighbor and a member of the National Guard went to the landing site to investigate. When they arrived they could not believe what they saw. Nestled on the hill was an object the size of a house and shaped like a globe. The witnesses described the object as pulsating. Their attention was suddenly drawn to a tree nearby, and believing that they were being watched by something, one of the group shone a flashlight at the tree. Then without warning a figure which the witnesses claimed to be at least 10 to 15 feet tall, with a blood red face and an odd glowing, greenish-orange eyes, floated down from the tree. The group quickly fled from the hillside, but upon later examination of the site, two parallel tracks and a large area of flattened grass were found, together with a foul, lingering smell.

NEW YORK DWARVES

On 24th April 1964, dairy farmer Gary T. Wilcox of Tioga County, New York, was about to receive the shock of his life. Two dwarves wearing seamless clothing, with hoods that covered their heads and faces, suddenly appeared in the field where he was working. Wilcox described them as being about 4 feet tall, and carrying a tray with soil samples, alfalfa

1961
EAGLE RIVER, WISCONSIN
EXTRATERRESTRIAL PANCAKES
Probably the most bizarre gift ever left by aliens has to be the pancakes given to plumber Joe Simonton in return for water. After giving three spacemen a jug, Simonton was rewarded with a number of pancakes before the UFO blazed off. Simonton later described the pancakes as rather "floury."

1963
BELO HORIZONTE, BRAZIL
ONE-EYED APPARITION
Three Brazilian boys were playing in their garden in the early evening when they saw an object floating in the air. One of the entities left the craft via a beam of light from the object's underside, and the boys were suddenly paralyzed. Much to their relief, the creature and craft shot off into the night.

1965
VALENSOLE, FRANCE
ET LAVENDER PICKERS
One July day, farmer Maurice Masse was walking through a vine-yard next to one of his lavender fields when he noticed a large, rugby ball-shaped craft. Beside the object were two small beings picking lavender. One of them paralyzed Masse with a stick, then got back in the craft and left.

• Artist's impression of a monster seen near a UFO by a group of children, Mrs Kathleen May and several others at Flatwoods, West Virginia, on 12th September 1952.

and grass cuttings. The creatures spoke to Wilcox in perfect English, explaining that they had come from Mars, and since they obtained their food from the atmosphere, they knew little about agriculture – and were here to learn. The conversation continued for hours, before the beings finally announced they had to go, but not before requesting another bag of fertilizer. They took off, and Wilcox quickly acquired a bag of fertilizer from his barn and placed it in the field. The following day, when he checked, the bag had gone. Later when asked if he thought that they had come back for the fertilizer he replied, "Well, anybody who would walk all the way to that field to get an 80 cent bag of fertilizer must be crazy."

AFTER ROSWELL

Possibly the first encounter with humanoid occupants after the notorious Roswell affair took place on 23rd July 1947, near Bauru, Brazil. José C. Higgins, who was working as part of a survey team, heard an ear-piercing whistle just prior to observing a huge discoid object land. Higgins claimed that it was made of a greyish metal, and was at least 150 feet in diameter. The object came to rest on curved legs, and seemed to have a wide rim around it. The remainder of the survey team all fled in terror, leaving Higgins to face the three 7 foot tall beings alone. Higgins described their attire as "Transparent suits covering head and body, and inflated like rubber bags, and they appeared to be carrying metal boxes."

The entities all looked alike, with huge round eyes and large round heads. They all lacked eyebrows, and their legs seemed to be longer in proportion to their bodies. The beings went on to show Higgins a diagram on the ground, which they made with a stick. Higgins presumed that the diagram, consisting of eight holes, was a depiction of a solar system with seven planets. The creatures then pointed to the outermost hole and indicated that this was called Orque, although it is not known whether they actually spoke to him or conveyed the message telepathically. The three beings then attempted to coax Higgins into their spaceship, but he

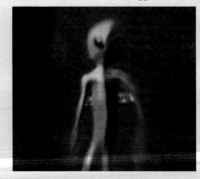

refused and eventually escaped to a nearby wood, where he watched them apparently playing, before they finally boarded their ship and disappeared towards the north.

1976

CANARY ISLANDS, SPAIN
GIANTS IN A SPHERE

Many eye-witnesses saw a spectacular UFO on the night of 22nd June, but three men also saw the occupants. The men claimed that they were confronted by a sphere hanging just a few feet from the road. Inside the transparent craft were two enormous beings operating a kind of control panel.

1992

BONNYBRIDGE, SCOTLAND
TARTAN UFO FLAP

One of the greatest UFO controversies the UK has ever witnessed continues to occur in the Scottish town of Bonnybridge. Hundreds of people have now witnessed UFOs in the region, with several craft being captured on camera and video recorder. There have also been reports of alien abductions.

1996

PILOZINHAS, BRAZIL
"LITTLE FANTASTIC MEN"

At the height of recent UFO sightings in Brazil, a 92-year-old farmer claimed that she was visited by "little fantastic men," who emerged from a spacecraft and began to speak to her in an unintelligible language. Unable to communicate, the little men stole some chickens before leaving in the UFO.

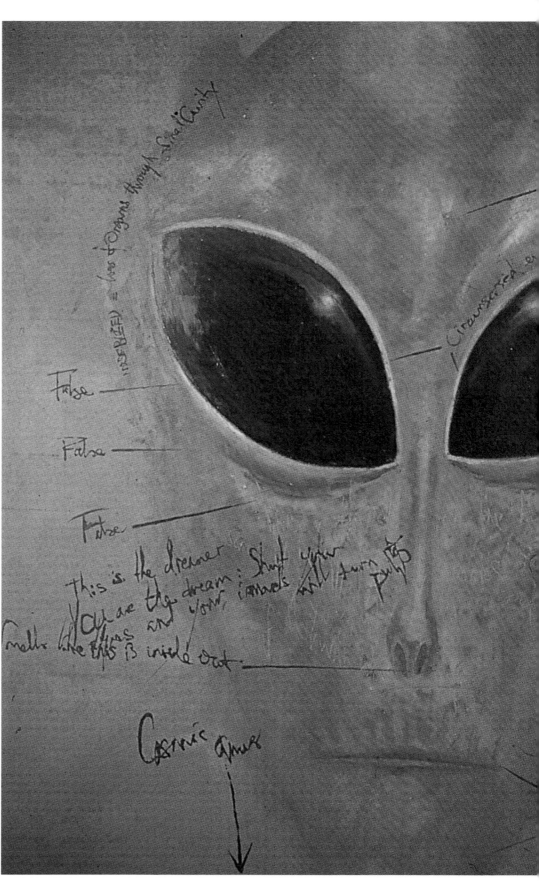

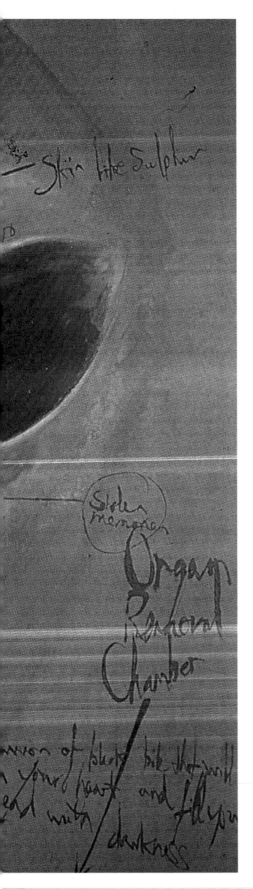

CHAPTER FOUR

CHAPTER FOUR
CLOSE ENCOUNTERS OF THE FOURTH KIND

INVOLUNTARY CONTACT WITH ALIENS IS ARGUABLY THE MOST compelling of all the five kinds of close encounter, and certainly the most emotive. What's so frightening about alien abductions and other kinds of forcible contact is the utter passivity of the victims – the subjects are quite literally snatched from their everyday lives by aliens and frequently, though not always, subjected to experiments to determine their physical characteristics. These experiments often focus on the human reproductive system, implying that aliens are particularly interested in the way the human race replicates itself: another, more sinister, explanation is that the abductors are 'harvesting' genetic matter, perhaps to create alien/human hybrids that can infiltrate the rest of society.

Yet it shouldn't be assumed that alien abductions are a purely modern phenomenon – they appear to have been happening for thousands of years, but were called something else. For example, everyone is familiar with stories of fairies, or little people, abducting children and even replacing them with their own. These stories bear many striking similarities to modern reports of alien abductions.

Victims of alien abduction often report similar experiences leading up to and during the event. The most common sensations include paralysis of the body, an inability to speak or cry out, being dazzled by a blinding bright light, hearing a crackling noise or sound similar to a dentist's drill and "losing" time. Many victims only realize they'd been abducted many years after the event, usually as a result of increasingly frequent flashbacks or health problems such as insomnia and depression. Of course, there are many "abductees" out there who appear to be shams, cynically exploiting the current interest in abductions for their own self-aggrandizement, but there are also some convincing reports from abductees who shun publicity.

While tales of alien abductions have been with us for centuries under different guises, a much more recent phenomenon are reports of child abductions and alien implants used as tracking devices. These tracking devices were only discovered when the victims were abducted again and the implants removed. Researcher Derrel Sims claims to have actually witnessed the surgical removal of such implants, which appear to be very strange small metallic devices.

CELEBRITY ABDUCTEES

THE MOST FAMOUS ABDUCTION OF RECENT times concerns Betty and Barney Hill, an otherwise perfectly ordinary American couple who revealed under hypnosis in 1964 that they'd been the subjects of experiments. The Hills claimed that while driving home from Canada on 19th September 1963, they observed a bright light near to the moon that seemed to be increasing in intensity. They stopped their car to get a better look at the light through binoculars, believing it to be an aircraft. The Hills continued their journey but soon noticed that the light was getting closer and closer. They stopped the car for a second time and once again viewed the craft through binoculars, this time describing it as "a big pancake with a row of windows," with at least a dozen occupants dressed in Nazi-style uniforms. The couple later heard two sets of beeping noises as they drove home. The Hills reported the incident to a local air force base and the National Investigative Committee on Aerial Phenomena, and it was only after closer investigation of the facts that the Hills realized the journey home had taken two hours longer than usual. Subsequent bouts of insomnia and depression persuaded the pair to undergo hypnotic regression, which revealed that they'd been abducted by the occupants of the craft they saw. Both were subjected to

● Betty and Barney Hill were the most famous abductees of the 1960s, but Barney in particular paid a heavy price. In addition to the stress of the experience, he was subjected to a barrage of tests and closely investigated by the government. Betty Hill is convinced that her husband's untimely death was expedited by his abduction.

BOTH WERE SUBJECTED TO FERTILITY TESTS AND SHOWN A MAP OF THE ALIENS' HOME, WHICH THEY CALLED ZETA RETICULI

● Barney Hill, seen here at a meeting of local UFO enthusiasts, with an illustration of the object which he and his wife encountered, prior to their abduction. The full details of their abduction experience did not surface until many months after their initial sighting.

fertility tests and shown a map of the aliens' home, which they called Zeta Reticuli. Barney died in 1969, some Ufologists believe as a result of his experience.

In the last two decades, the two most celebrated alien contacts concern Travis Walton and Whitley Streiber, again both Americans. Unlike the Hills, their stories have been turned into Hollywood movies: Walton's in *Fire in the Sky* and Streiber's in *Communion*. Although both men readily admit that Hollywood treated their stories with a great deal of artistic license, playing down some elements and exaggerating others, their own account of events is still pretty startling.

• Travis Walton points to the exact spot where he claims he was abducted by a UFO in the White Mountains of Arizona. Unlike other abductions, it seems Walton was only taken because he ventured near the craft, while the rest of his colleagues fled. Although Walton was subjected to distressing experiments, he has reported no long-term side effects.

THE TRAVIS WALTON STORY

Back in 1975, Walton was an ordinary logger working as part of a seven-man team in the White Mountains of Arizona. The loggers had just finished a hard day's work and were heading back to town along a primitive dirt track. The first thing they noticed was a light emanating through the trees. They all initially thought that a small plane might have crashed into the forest, but soon realized that it was a metallic "disk" lighting up the whole area. Walton, fearing that the object would disappear

WAS WALTON LYING?

Arch US skeptic Phillip Klass believes that the whole Walton affair was an elaborate hoax perpetrated by the logging team. He has discovered that the team were contracted to clear a section of forest, and that they had fallen behind with the work. Klass heard that the company paying the contract had written in a penalty clause, whereby any delays to the work would result in considerable financial penalties. Klass concludes that the team leader, Mike Rogers, approached the other team members, and together they concocted a story which could not be proven either way in an attempt to escape the terms of the contract. What Klass cannot account for, however, is the simple fact that Travis did actually disappear, and when he returned he was indeed deeply traumatized. Yet it's interesting to note that the contractors did back down on the penalty clause as a result of Walton's disappearance.

With Six Other Witnesses
Walton Claims UFO Sighting

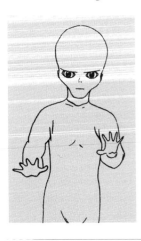

• Travis Walton's impressions of what he claims to have encountered that fateful day in the White Mountains. The first picture shows one of the creatures that were responsible for his abduction. The second picture shows the alien spacecraft aboard which Walton was subjected to a degrading ordeal at the hands of the "Grey" aliens.

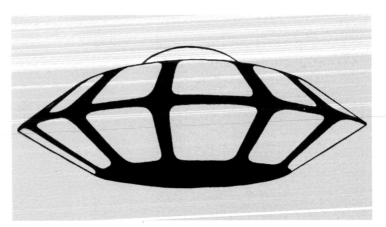

- Many thousands of people from all walks of life, and living in every country on the planet, have reported being abducted, by a varying assortment of alien beings. These three pictures are artists' impressions of what alien visitors may look like. The images were created after drawing upon a wealth of eye-witness information and testimony from the very people in the position to know – namely the victims of alien abduction themselves.

before he could get a closer look, leapt out of the truck and rushed up to it. Suddenly afraid, Walton tried to get back to his companions, but was struck by a blue beam of light from the disk which knocked him to the ground. The next thing he remembered was going numb before passing out. Walton's colleagues, presuming he was dead, fled in panic. Later, they returned to the scene, only to find that the disk was heading off towards the north east, and that Walton's body had vanished.

Not surprisingly, the police became involved, and suspicion fell on Walton's colleagues. They were subjected to lie-detector tests to find out if they'd killed him, while the woodland area was carefully searched for any sign of the body. Then, five days after disappearing, Walton turned up again. Extensive medical and psychiatric tests merely showed that he had lost 11 pounds in weight, mostly water, although urine samples indicated that he had not been starved. This is his account of what happened to him on the ship, which came out during hypnotic regression sessions:

"I was lying on a table, on my back and in pain. I found it hard to breathe and drifted in and out of

THE ABDUCTION EXPERIENCE

During the "classic" abduction, the abductee is laid out on a table, often within a white room, and restrained or paralyzed. An examination is carried out over the oral, anal and genital areas by small, grey, humanoids with large black oval eyes. Samples of sperm or ova are often removed.

Many female abductees believe they have had fetuses implanted and then removed later by aliens, and that the aliens have a scheme for hybrid alien/human repopulation. Some abductees have bonded very profoundly with their abductors, who are often

I WAS LYING ON A TABLE, ON MY BACK AND IN PAIN. I FOUND IT HARD TO BREATHE AND DRIFTED IN AND OUT OF CONSCIOUSNESS. WHEN I DID FOCUS THERE WERE CREATURES STANDING OVER ME

consciousness. When I did focus there were creatures standing over me. I became hysterical, jumped off the table and hit one of the creatures, although I was very weak. They extended their hands towards me – they were smaller than me and had long heads with dark eyes." Eventually, the group left, and Walton fled into a smaller room where he reported seeing stars and symbols moving around the walls. He continues:

"Something made me turn around. I saw a man standing in a doorway, he had a helmet on and he took me out of the craft into a much larger place, with a more natural air. There were various different disks lined up in there. Three very tall men with blonde hair and piercing blue eyes tried to subdue me and put a mask over my mouth. The next thing I knew I was lying on the highway ... near my local town, and the craft quickly and silently went up in

• The harvesting of ova, perhaps to create a hybrid race, is frequently reported by female abductees.

the air and disappeared. I eventually managed to call my family. I only learned later that I had been gone for five whole days, I had presumed it was all in one night. At the time I was frightened and confused and I presumed the aliens were hostile, but in retrospect I'm not so sure ..."

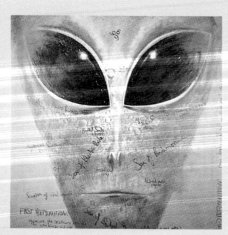

reported to have telepathically informed the abductees that they love them and will

not harm them. This has even led to sexual attraction to the abductors. In contrast, many abductees suffer from symptoms akin to that of rape victims, due to forced interference with their sexual organs.

Is It Real?

Considering that a recent nationwide survey revealed that 5% of the American population believed they had been abducted, and claims of abduction are on the increase world-wide, it is hard to ignore the subject and even harder to claim it has no substance.

• Mysterious scarring, believed to be caused by a UFO light beam.

WHITLEY STREIBER'S COMMUNION

Fire in the Sky, Hollywood's version of Walton's story, was followed by a marked increase in reports of alien abductions, but the impact of *Communion* has been even greater. This movie depicted the "Greys," the aliens that Whitley Streiber is convinced have been in regular contact with him since 1989. Streiber's story is very different from Walton's as he claims the aliens came to him. And while Walton remembers very physical sensations from the abduction, Streiber's contact took place on a much more cerebral, spiritual level. In a recent interview with the British magazine *UFO Reality*, Streiber expanded on the reasons the Greys have been contacting him. "What they have to offer is the shock itself, primarily. The shock of the contact experience ... is worth having in the sense that this shock cracks, as it were, your personal paradigm. It causes you to be able to see beyond the ordinary mechanical level of the universe, to see beyond the dynamics of Newtonian physics, if you will." Streiber's determination to explain the encounters in exalted, spiritual terms has led to many skeptics accusing him of fabricating the stories in an attempt to revive his flagging career as a science fiction writer. Yet Streiber has undergone three different lie-detector tests, as well as extensive neurological examinations to check whether he was hallucinating as a result of temporal-lobe epilepsy. All these tests were negative, and Streiber maintains that he's been in contact with spiritually advanced Grey aliens ...

LOST WAS THE KEY

In the bizarre world of alien abductions, there are many differing descriptions of the beings, spacecraft and procedures involved. However, Leah Haley's story is unlike anything heard before.

Haley claims to have suffered a lifetime of alien visitations stretching as far back as her childhood. The beings responsible for Haley's abductions fit the classic description of "Grey" aliens, although she remembers their color as being more off-white than grey, similar to an eggshell hue. These beings have large, black, almond-shaped eyes, two slits for a nose and an indistinguishable mouth. They do not have any body hair and have four digits as opposed to our five. The beings spoke to Haley on several occasions via telepathy, but strangest of all, they actually told her some of the reasons why they were abducting humans.

She was informed that they were performing genetic experiments on their human victims. During Haley's abductions she was subjected to medical examinations by the creatures. She had tissue and ova samples removed, and it was during these surgical procedures that she was informed of the purpose of the sampling.

Although Haley was beginning to recall conscious memories of various abduction scenarios that appeared to have taken place during the 1970s and 1980s, at the time she did not know what to think or do about the encounters. She had never heard of alien abduction before, and was not particularly interested in the UFO phenomenon. Haley attempted to convince herself that the experience was just a lucid dream, especially as it had happened at night time, although the whole affair was as clear as two people talking to one another.

She had no context in which to place the experience, but was able to recognize what happened to her as alien abduction by undergoing hypnotic regression with John Carpenter, an abduction researcher in Springfield, Missouri, and head of abduction research for the Mutual UFO Network (MUFON).

ENCOUNTER IN THE WOODS

Under regression, Haley was able to make sense of an early childhood encounter in the woods with her brother and a friend. It transpired that when the threesome, together with the boy's father, had scattered out and searched for the spacecraft which

• Leah Haley's story is one of the most spectacular accounts of not only alien abduction, but also military intervention.

they had sighted, Haley did in fact come across a being in the woods. The creature, a typical "Grey" alien which Haley had remembered seeing consciously on other occasions, led her through the woods until they came upon a clearing.

In the clearing there was a round spacecraft which appeared to be hovering inches off the ground. A ray of light shot out of the craft and beamed Haley and the being aboard the ship. Once on board she could remember having her arms and legs poked and examined using a long thin instrument. Unfortunately, that was the best that Haley could manage under hypnosis, and she was unable to recall how she got back to the woods. In addition, she later recalled an incident in 1991 when she was abducted by the same big black-eyed creatures, but this time they did something totally different. In the past, Haley had always been taken back to the place that she was abducted from, be it her home or more specifically her bedroom, but on this occasion she was not. Instead, she was abandoned in a field near to her home, where she stood disoriented by drugs which had been administered by the aliens. Suddenly a military helicopter landed close by. Men wearing military uniforms leapt from the helicopter carrying M-16 rifles. She was quickly ushered into the helicopter and transported to a military base.

Once at the base, Haley was whisked into a conference room and given an injection in the arm. Tranquilized, all that Haley can remember being told by the man in charge of the military unit was not to tell anybody that she had seen a spaceship. He warned that if she did, he would "terminate" her, but to date, this threat has not been carried out.

FAIRY FOLK, OR ALIENS?

Could it be possible that modern day accounts of alien abduction are comparable to stories of fairies?

The following anecdote has much in common with the classic alien abduction. It was recorded in 1887, by the Rev. Elias Owen, and concerns a servant called David Williams.

Williams was on his way home one evening to the house where he worked in North Wales, closely following his mistress. The lady of the house, believing Williams to be behind her, continued home and didn't look back. To her great surprise, he did not arrive back at the house until three hours later. On questioning Williams about his disappearance, he was insistent that he had arrived only minutes after her. He kept to his story until eventually he conceded that something may have been amiss, and promptly recalled a string of bizarre events.

Williams claimed that he had seen a comet flying through the sky, and close behind it was what he described as a "hoop of fire," with a small man and woman standing within it. When the object landed, the two beings quickly leapt from the hoop and began to construct a circle on the ground. After their task was finished a group of fairy folk appeared from nowhere and began to dance around the circle, accompanied by the sweetest music Williams had ever heard. He also noticed that the whole area was awash in an eerie light. In time, the meteor returned, picked up the two small beings, and shot off skyward, and the remaining little people simply vanished.

Williams found himself once again in the dark, and proceeded home, thinking that he had only stopped to watch

for a few minutes. These events are remarkably akin to a modern day abduction, the only difference being that Williams lived at a time when fairies were widely observed – and, of course, alien abduction was totally unheard of. What was suspected, however, was that fairies stole children or created hybrids, which again echoes the modern stories of alien abduction.

ALIEN ABDUCTOR PHOTO?

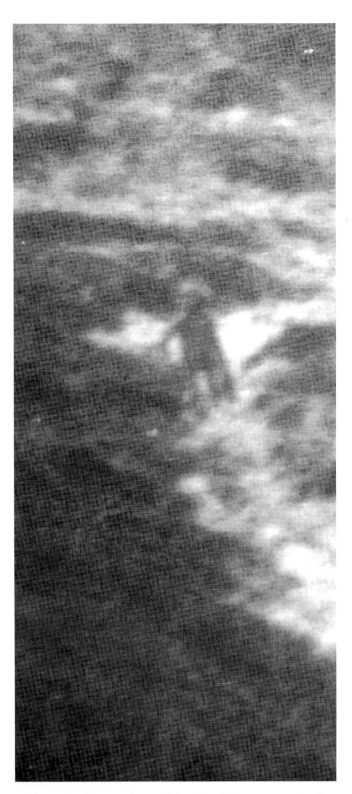

• This is the famous photo of the Ilkley Moor entity, taken by former police officer Alan Godfrey.

THE CASE OF THE ILKLEY MOOR ALIEN IS one of the most controversial cases of alien abduction recorded in the UK, mainly because of the furore surrounding a photograph taken of the abductor. A former police officer, Alan Godfrey, claimed that on the morning of 1st December 1987, he disturbed a small green humanoid while crossing Ilkley Moor in the northern county of Yorkshire. Surprised, the creature ran away, before halting at a safe distance and apparently signalling to the officer by bending and raising its right arm. The officer, who was carrying a pocket camera to take photos of the town of Ilkley, snapped the startled entity before it ran off to a large rock formation.

As the police officer followed the mysterious creature, he came across a dome-topped, sleek, silver metallic disk. In a fraction of a second, the flying saucer rose at breathtaking speed and disappeared high into the clouds.

ODD ENCOUNTERS ON THE MOORS

Other, equally strange encounters have taken place on Ilkley Moor. Only a quarter of a mile from where Alan Godfrey claimed he was abducted, is a group of outcropping rocks called the Cow and Calf. In the summer of 1987, a local couple were driving nearby when they spotted a mass of white lights hovering in the vicinity of the rocks. More recently, on 30th March 1996, a member of the UFO research group BEAMS (British Earth Aerial Mystery Society) reported a paranormal experience near the "swastika," or Fylfot Stone. Mark Gibbons, along with other members of his family, had walked up to this intriguing piece of coarse sandstone which measures about 19 feet long and about 4 feet thick. Upon touching the stone, which has long been associated with strange powers, Gibbons claimed he suddenly felt energy rushing through his body. Almost immediately, the nagging pain of an old arthritic complaint vanished. His aunt, a self-proclaimed psychic, then proceeded to meditate and begin a conversation with what she described as an unseen entity on the rock. Suddenly, Gibbons saw a stunning, glowing, violet-colored "vision" shoot out from the swastika-like device carved on the rock. Although the vision quickly disappeared, Gibbons is adamant that he did not hallucinate. In addition to the

If this story wasn't strange enough, there were other discrepancies. For example, the officer seemed unable to account for two hours following his encounter. The blurred photo and negative of the alien raising its right arm (see opposite) were subsequently examined by Kodak, which declared that the images had not been tampered with.

About a week after the event, the police officer also noticed that the polarity of his compass had been reversed, so that it now pointed south. The compass was examined at the University of Manchester's Institute of Science and Technology, who concluded that the only kind of magnet which would have this effect on a compass would be a very powerful, Japanese-made model – which was commercially unavailable at the time of the encounter – or a rapidly applied or "pulsed" magnetic field generated by electricity.

Worried about the missing two hours and recurring dreams of a starry sky, Alan Godfrey later underwent hypnotic regression. Godfrey revealed that he chanced upon the the hovering silver disk and was levitated inside the craft. His captors were described

AFTER BEING EXAMINED BY AN ILLUMINATED SCANNING DEVICE, GODFREY WAS SHOWN HARROWING IMAGES OF THE EARTH'S ENVIRONMENTAL DESTRUCTION, AS WELL AS ANOTHER FILM HE ABSOLUTELY REFUSED TO DISCUSS

as having green, roughish-looking skin, and were of small stature, "about 4 foot, with big pointed ears and large black eyes ... with three big fingers, like sausages." After being examined by an illuminated scanning device, Godfrey was shown harrowing images of the Earth's environmental destruction, as well as another film he absolutely refused to discuss as he'd been sworn to secrecy. Finally, Godfrey revealed he had taken the photo at the end of the encounter, leading to speculation that he captured a shot of the alien waving goodbye.

mystery of the swastika, there are also various stone circles on Ilkley Moor, the best known of which is the "12 Apostles." Several photographers of this site have reported anomalous glows and distortions on their prints.

Furthermore, BEAMS claims it has uncovered evidence of some kind of military radio-delay building on Ilkley Moor. Mark Gibbons and fellow researcher/archaeologist Gary Foster reportedly stumbled across an installation surrounded by a double wire-mesh perimeter fence, comprising of two large steel masts like radio pylons, with equipment housings at their bases. They also found what looked like a guard tower adjacent to the main area, covering an entrance to the compound. Numerous satellite-type

dishes were clustered around the lower portion of the two steel towers. After speaking with an ex-communication/radar officer of the Royal Air Force, Foster concludes that the double perimeter fence is a standard security set up for many communications sites in remote areas. "However, the guard tower at the entrance to the installation compound is unusual. If it is a guard tower, why? What for? These are rather over-elaborate security measures for the middle of nowhere. It also had a manually operated swivel-mounted micro-transceiver dish attached to the tower. What is this for? And why at this installation? The masts themselves appear to be of a standard type. The satellite micro-transceiver dishes are commonplace and do not indicate anything other than an advantageous location."

The British Ministry of Defence has neither confirmed nor denied that there is some kind of military communications site at Ilkley Moor. Whatever the real purpose of the mysterious building BEAMS came across, Ilkley Moor remains one of the most alluring sites in British UFO lore. What's particularly intriguing is the link between anomalous phenomena and ancient monuments: another historical site, Maiden Castle near Dorchester in the county of Dorset, also yields large numbers of UFO sightings, as do numerous Iron Age stone circles in the county of Wiltshire (also home to Stonehenge and some of the most impressive crop circles seen in the UK).

• The swastika rock on Ilkley Moor, where some amazing paranormal phenomena have been recorded.

HAVE YOU BEEN ABDUCTED?

NOW THAT ALIEN ABDUCTIONS HAVE such a hold over our imagination, several common anomalies have emerged among abductees in general. These anomalies are so common that they are even used to differentiate between real and false claims of abduction. Certainly, there are plenty of false claims, as the greedy or attention-seeking try to capitalize on the current interest in alien abduction.

Time and time again, it's been revealed that the victims of alien abduction rarely have an insight into the exact events of their abduction experience. However, hypnotic regression can supposedly relax the mind to such an extent that these subconscious memories are gently released.

It should be noted at this point that relatively little is known about hypnotic regression. As this is the main means of recalling abduction memories, we should perhaps be careful not to assume it is a watertight method and that regressionists all reach the same standards of integrity. After all, it is possible to place a suggestion during or prior to regression.

Although hypnotic regression is the main recollection technique employed in abduction cases, most abductees already have a nagging sense that something paranormal has happened to them, before they are hypnotized. It is this disturbing uneasiness which motivates them to seek regression therapy in the first place.

It is perhaps encouraging to see from the study of the paranormal in general that there are very interesting correlations to some aspects of alien abduction and the paranormal phenomenon of out of body experience (OBE) and even near death experience (NDE). If you are wondering whether you have ever been abducted by aliens, then there are definite clues to look for. The following list is, of course, only a guide for the curious. Alternative natural explanations are offered, such as repeated out of body experiences or simply hallucination, but when all of the following attributes occur, the odds seem stacked in favor of a paranormal experience. If the last ten years is anything to go by, the frequency of alien abduction reports certainly looks set to increase exponentially.

ABDUCTION CLUES

1: SIGHTING A UFO

Whether the subject is randomly chosen or sought specifically for abduction we can only guess, but sighting a UFO is often the first indication of an imminent abduction, and more often than not the starting point in hypnotic regression, before the whole story unfolds. In British abductions, there seem to be two very common types of UFO which are sighted just before the victims lose all sense of time: the black triangular UFO, similar to those sighted in Belgium in 1990 and the traditional silver reflective flying saucer.

Alternative Explanation

Many UFOs are not unexplained at all – they are in fact conventional aircraft sighted from strange angles. Also responsible for many UFO sightings are meteors, balloons, satellites or shooting stars, although it is evident that not all UFOs can be categorized quite so readily.

2: EXPERIENCE OF INTENSE LIGHT

This light is most often blue, sometimes green and very bright. It usually strikes the forehead.

Alternative Explanation

This could be caused by epilepsy, which is sometimes preceded by this characteristic vision of intense light.

- Abductees often report that their experience was preceded by a blinding light. This light can either act as a tranquilizer, paralyzing the entire body, or can have an extremely calming effect on other witnesses.

3: CRACKLING NOISES

An unusual, possibly internal, crackling noise in the ear, also noted in OBEs, seems to repeat itself at an ever-increasing rate during the abduction, until the next phase of the experience occurs.

Alternative Explanation

Electromagnetic energy can cause high-pitched noises and feelings of fear, although this explanation could equally be applied in favor of alien abduction, as electromagnetic energy is linked to UFO activity.

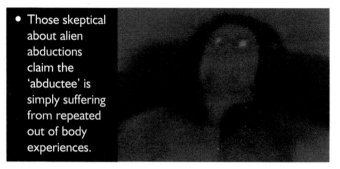

- Those skeptical about alien abductions claim the 'abductee' is simply suffering from repeated out of body experiences.

4: OBE – OUT OF BODY EXPERIENCE

Usually described as floating above the bed or above the position where your physical body is suspended, in a "spirit-like" state.

Alternative Explanation

This could be a vivid lucid dream, or a dream state where you remain very aware within your dream environment. However, this is hard to accept when dream surroundings are identical to actual surroundings.

5: NIGHT SEIZURES AND PARALYSIS

These night seizures prevent speech or movement and yet the victim can still be conscious. What is interesting is the correlation between night seizures and OBEs. The victim remembers floating in paralysis away from where they are sleeping, sometimes moving through solid objects such as walls. In an abduction scenario, this is sometimes akin to the "tractor beam," a beam of energy which tows the person up into a spacecraft for closer examination.

Alternative Explanation

Night seizures could simply be caused by a paralyzing hormone which your body secretes during sleep to prevent you from acting out your dreams and injuring yourself.

POST-ABDUCTION CHARACTERISTICS

1: LOST TIME

Abduction victims experience loss of awareness of what happened, usually within a time frame of a matter of hours, although some people experience time loss within minutes.

Often, this loss of time is instantly recognizable; abductees have reported glancing at their watch twice within a few seconds and noticing a dramatic lapse in time. This discrepancy has even been revealed to people while they're driving. Loss of time is one of the most common characteristics of alien abduction reports and as such deserve much more study.

Alternative Explanation

Time loss could be attributed to a fit or type of epilepsy (such as temporal-lobe epilepsy), although most abductees have no history of this ailment. It would not be applicable to some cases, such as driving whilst being abducted, unless the car managed to drive itself for a couple of hours.

2: SCREEN MEMORY

When trying to remember events within the lost time, abductees have a strong image of something that has nothing to do with aliens or UFOs and cannot comprehend why. This is often referred to as an implanted screen memory. Abductees will frequently experience a strong image, yet will be confused as to why they are remembering it and exactly when it occurred.

Alternative Explanation

The memory could have simply blanked out, which would explain the missing time.

3: NOSE BLEEDS AND SCARS

Mysterious nose bleeds and scarring, such as the mysterious marks that appeared on British abductee Pauline Delcour-Minn (above), may eventually be accounted for in regression or remembered during abduction. These symptoms could be the result of being medically examined by aliens. Nose bleeds can occur due to implants which certain Ufologists, such as Derrel Sims, claim to have seen surgically removed. When analyzed, these implants have shown a strange mineral composition.

Alternative Explanation

The source of the injury is natural.

4: VIVID DREAMS

Abductees suffer vivid memories and dreams of alien

8BC

ISRAEL
ANCIENT ASTRONAUT

The biblical character Enoch is thought by many researchers of the ancient astronaut theory to be the first written example of an alien abduction, who is quite simply not returned. Not only did he "walk with God," but unlike many other abduction victims, he is presumably still walking with him now.

6BC

HOLY LAND
JACOB'S LADDER

In the Old Testament, Jacob dreamt of a ladder that reached down from Heaven; upon the ladder were angels traveling up and down. When he awoke he heard a voice telling him that his seed would be spread across the earth. Could this "seed" have been implanted by aliens?

1957

FRANCISCO DE SALES, BRAZIL
FORCED ALIEN INTERCOURSE

Brazilian Antonio Villas Boas reported in October 1965 that he'd been abducted by aliens some eight years earlier and forced to copulate with a female. Boas recalled being covered in a thick liquid, and that the female alien had blonde hair, a wide face, a pointed chin and blue eyes. He had sex twice.

- Police officer Alan Godfrey, above, was the victim of one of the best-publicized abduction cases in the UK. Godfrey allegedly encountered a small "Green Entity" while out walking on Ilkley Moor, in the county of Yorkshire. He managed to capture the creature on camera, which waved goodbye as it headed off towards its spacecraft.

beings, which usually reveal the image of a small grey humanoid figure with large black eyes. Such strong images usually cause trauma and anxiety when recalled or viewed in an illustration. For those who have not been regressed or have little idea of why they should fear the image, this can become a very confusing and disturbing time. Sometimes the fear is related solely to the two oval black eyes.

Alternative Explanation
Eyes are particularly emotive. A fear of black eyes could come about from a fear of insects such as wasps, or a fear of skulls and their link with death.

5: OBSESSIVE PURSUIT OF UFO KNOWLEDGE
Abduction victims feel compelled to deepen their understanding of UFO and alien phenomena, to the point of obsession.

Alternative Explanation
UFOs are a fascinating enigma and the feverish pursuit of further information may be only natural.

6: INSOMNIA
Insomnia, the inability to fall asleep, can become particularly acute around the early hours of the morning. This is also a time when UFO sightings are remarkably common. Subconscious fear of sleep could be linked with the trauma of night abductions, or the possibility that abductions are related to OBEs – which usually happen just prior to sleep.

Alternative Explanation
This can be explained by a fear of the dark, fear of the unknown, or perhaps an irrational fear of imagined aliens. Hyperactive or generally stressed individuals usually find they cannot sleep.

7: HEIGHTENED SPIRITUAL AWARENESS
After contact with UFOs and aliens, a sense of spirituality is sometimes rekindled, which is comparable to religious conviction. In extreme cases, psychic ability is demonstrated, whereby people claim to be able to link telepathically with others.

Alternative Explanation
Ufology can be viewed as a new religion, since traditional religions have lost appeal to the "baby boom" generation. Could the hunger for a meaning to life be satisfied through belief in aliens, with their supposed interest in our spiritual growth?

1964
FRODSHAM, ENGLAND
TOTAL RECALL
On 28th July, Pauline Delcour-Minn was walking down a quiet lane, when she suddenly found herself on her hands and knees in a field with no recollection of how she had gotten there. Nearly 30 years later, she recalled through regression that she had been abducted. She still bears the scars.

1967
MADAGASCAR
LEGIONNAIRES ABDUCTED
A French Foreign Legionnaire known only as Wolff claimed his platoon was abducted by a bright metallic object which looked like a "shining egg." Three hours mysteriously disappeared, and for up to three days afterwards the soldiers suffered chronic headaches and disturbing flashbacks.

1973
PASCAGOULA, MISSISSIPPI
SHIPYARD ABDUCTION
Shipyard worker Charles Hickson claimed to have been abducted by a large egg-shaped spacecraft while fishing on the Pascagoula river. Under hypnotic regression, he described his abductors as creatures about 5 feet tall, with wrinkled grey skin, long arms, but no necks or eyes.

Sexual Probing and Alien Implants

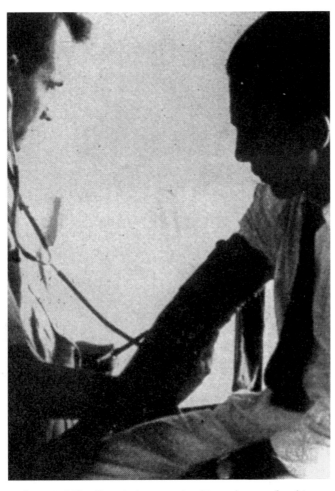

• Antonio Villas Boas being examined by a doctor after his sexual encounter with alien beings. He speculates that he impregnated the alien with whom he had sex twice.

ONE OF THE MOST COMMONLY TOUTED theories surrounding the abduction of human beings by alien races is that they are attempting to clone a super race. In some cases, the abductee is actually forced to have sexual intercourse with alien beings; possibly the best example of this unearthly liaison is the case of Antonio Villas Boas of Brazil. Boas claims that at 1:00 am on 15 October 1957, he was plowing a field with his tractor, when a luminous egg-shaped object, which Boas described as about 35 feet long and 23 feet wide, landed nearby. Three metal legs came down from under the craft, and Boas's tractor lights and engine went dead. Four figures wearing helmets emerged from the object and dragged Boas up the ladder of the craft and on board. Once inside, Boas encountered other humanoid figures who communicated in "a series of barks, slightly resembling the sounds made by a dog." The creatures were about 5 feet tall and dressed in skin-tight overalls. Boas was then stripped naked, and a blood sample was taken from his chin. He did not feel any pain during this procedure. A little while later a beautiful naked woman entered the room and seduced Boas into having sex with her twice. "Shortly after we had separated, the door opened," Boas said. "One of the men appeared on the threshold and called the woman. Then she went out. But, before going out, she turned to me, pointed at her belly and then pointed towards me and with a smile (or something like it), she finally pointed

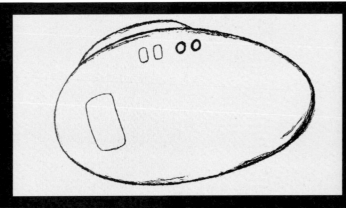

1975
NEW MEXICO
SILVERY UFO MAKES CONTACT
On 13th August 1975, US Air Force Sergeant Charles L. Moody revealed under hypnotic regression he was abducted by two beings from a silvery UFO he spotted during a meteor shower. They told Moody that further contact with humans would not be made for another 20 years.

1977
RIO DE JANEIRO, BRAZIL
ROBOT ALIENS
Antonio La Rubia claims to have been abducted by alien beings near the town of Paciencia, Brazil, in October of this year. He described the creatures as emotionless beings who moved like robots. His drawing of the alien (right), although rather basic, does resemble other entities encountered.

A BEAUTIFUL NAKED WOMAN ENTERED THE ROOM AND SEDUCED BOAS INTO HAVING SEX WITH HER TWICE.

towards the sky – I think it was in the direction of the south."

Boas was then handed back his clothing, minus his lighter, and given a tour of the craft, which he remembered with great accuracy. He described in particular the "dish-shaped cupola" overhead that whistled like the "sound of air being drawn in by a vacuum cleaner" as it revolved. Finally his guide pointed towards the ladder, and Boas left the craft.

● An artist's impression shows the intensity of the struggle which Boas put up prior to his abduction.

The bewildered farmer then watched as the object shot off like a bullet. Boas was later examined by Dr Olavo Fontes for ailments which appeared to resemble radiation poisoning; during the examination, Fontes noticed two small dark scars on Boas's chin and lesions on his body. The doctor concluded that Boas might have had a case of radiation poisoning.

Why would alien races be interested in cross-breeding with humans? One theory suggests that the aliens are in need of something which we have and that they long to possess – emotion. It is a common belief that some of the races visiting this planet are bereft of emotion: they go about their examinations in a clinical manner, almost as if they had been pre-programed. They find it hard to comprehend human emotions such as joy, sorrow and pain, and that is why some of the examinations are carried out without anesthetic. Another possibility is that the aliens' own race is in jeopardy and that by creating a

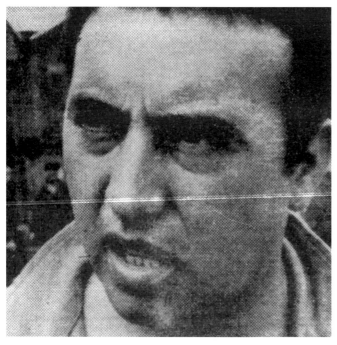

● The case of Antonio Villas Boas is believed to be one of the earliest documented abductions, occuring in 1957. Forty years on, the phenomenon is increasing rapidly.

1989
MANHATTAN, NEW YORK
THE CORTILE ABDUCTION
In November 1989, Linda Cortile claims that she was abducted from her apartment by aliens. She recalls floating out of the window of her apartment and into a UFO. Even more bizarrely, an eye-witness was found who claimed to have seen the whole incident from the street below.

1996
SOUTHAMPTON, ENGLAND
STOLEN GENETIC MATERIAL
A woman claimed to have been taken from her bedroom by "Grey" aliens. Under hypnosis, she recalled experiments where a tube was placed in her navel, and during regression therapy revealed that she was abducted every seven years. The experiment suggests the aliens were taking her ova.

hybrid race they may somehow be able to save themselves. Perhaps they are nearing a time when they will attempt to settle on this planet, but cannot survive in our atmosphere, but by splicing genes they are able to create a new generation capable of being able to withstand the atmosphere.

The third, and possibly the hardest theory to swallow, is that these creatures are our creators. US researchers Zecharia Sitchin and Marc Davenport are convinced that alien races may have had a hand in our development, and that in our ancient history, we worshipped them as gods. Alien abductions are simply check-ups on our biological evolution. Although this final hypothesis seems at first to be a little far-fetched, if we look at some of the more desirable after-effects of alien abduction, we may find some clues. One common denominator in most abduction cases is a heightened spiritual awareness, as well as increased psychic abilities. Marc Davenport claims that in most cases of alien abduction, the witness states that communication is made via telepathy, an ability which disappears in humans from childhood onwards. However, when the aliens converse in this manner to humans, they are awakening a dormant capability, and this is why abductees invariably claim to have been given psychic powers.

• Derrel Sims

Implants – Proof at Last

In a world that is constantly striving for answers, one man has come forward with what he claims is irrefutable proof that aliens do exist, and that they are abducting humans. Furthermore, he has the evidence quite literally in the palm of his hand – his name is Derrel Sims.

Sims is a well respected abduction researcher and hypnotherapist from the US who claims to have assisted in the removal of alien implants from two abductees. He recently oversaw a surgical operation by Dr Roger Leir, to remove the said implants. Sims and Leir first met at a UFO conference in California in 1995, where Sims was showing X-rays claiming to show an alien implant placed in an abductee's foot. Leir initially believed the X-rays to show a stainless steel suture present after the foot had undergone a surgical procedure involving the bone. However, Sims informed Leir that no surgery had ever been performed, despite the fact that the

ALIEN RACES MAY HAVE HAD A HAND IN OUR DEVELOPMENT, AND THAT IN OUR ANCIENT HISTORY, WE WORSHIPPED THEM AS GODS. ALIEN ABDUCTIONS ARE SIMPLY CHECK-UPS ON OUR BIOLOGICAL EVOLUTION

X-ray showed an obvious foreign body on either side of the big toe. After a few weeks, a second abductee was introduced to Leir by Sims with similar objects in his hand, which had been confirmed by X-rays.

A team of fully qualified surgeons performed the operations to remove the implants from the two witnesses – a man and a woman – while the entire procedure was filmed. Leir made his initial incision on the inside of the big toe, and it took nearly a whole hour before he found the first foreign body. The object was greyish in colour, and Leir carefully clamped the object and removed it from the surrounding tissue, and placed it onto gauze for a thorough examination. It was triangular in shape and very tiny indeed, measuring about 1 by $\frac{1}{4}$ inches. Dr Leir then

• This is a close up of an alien implant that Dr Roger Leir removed from an abductee. Aliens are thought to use these implants as tracking and monitoring devices, which may account for multiple abduction scenarios.

- This X-ray clearly shows a foreign body near the center of an abductee's hand. Derrel Sims believes it is an implant.

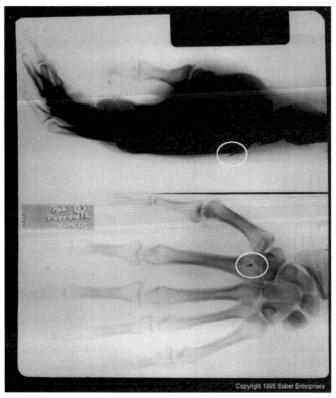

Copyright 1995 Saber Enterprises

IN THE TISSUES SURROUNDING THE IMPLANTS THERE WERE NUMEROUS NERVE ENDINGS WHICH SHOULD NOT HAVE BEEN THERE

attempted to remove the second object from the other side of the big toe, which he succeeded in doing, although this took a little longer as the object was a lot smaller than the first. Both implants were extensively examined, and a strange membrane was found to be surrounding the objects, which could not be scraped off, even with a surgical knife.

Attention then turned to the second patient, with the implant in the hand, and on this occasion Dr Leir acted as an assistant to a fellow surgeon. Again the surgery was a success and an object, almost identical to the second object removed from the big toe of the first patient, was discovered and extracted.

The Findings

The membranes which could not be scraped off were dried and removed, revealing a black, shiny metallic core which seemed to be magnetic. These objects are

IMAGINARY FRIENDS

The recent upsurge in reported alien abductions has led many researchers to delve deeper into the subject. In the US, it's become common for researchers to investigate the abductee's childhood. It is now widely believed that alien contact is initiated with the abductee from the age of four upwards, and proof for this hypothesis is slowly coming to light. Abductees are now being urged to regress further back to their adolescence in order to supply further clues to this puzzling enigma; one possible pointer to alien intervention is the existence of "imaginary friends." Most people have had an imaginary friend at some stage, even if they do not remember it. Some psychical researchers now believe that children who are seeing spirits, rather than aliens, as pre-adolescents are remarkably sensitive to paranormal phenomena. One British researcher, Pauline Delcour-Minn – also a hypnotic regressionist and self-proclaimed abductee – has even gone as far as to suggest that we have all been abducted by aliens at some stage, and that the pact which allows them to do this is agreed in the mother's womb.

now being subjected to extensive scientific testing. Tissues that were removed from the area surrounding the objects were sent to pathology for analysis, revealing that while there were numerous peripheral nerves and pressure receptors, there was no evidence of inflammation, either acute or chronic, no inflammatory cells or infiltrates, and no fibrosis.

"I told Dr Leir the day before surgery that if these objects are alien-related, then no inflammatory cells would be present, acute or chronic, but there would be lots of the wrong kind of nerve cells," Sims said. "As soon as the [pathology] reports came back with the non-inflammatory response and the wrong nerve cells, Leir asked 'how could you possibly have known this?' He'd previously said inflammatory cells would always be present."

If Sims and Leir really have removed implants, proof of alien abduction is finally at hand.

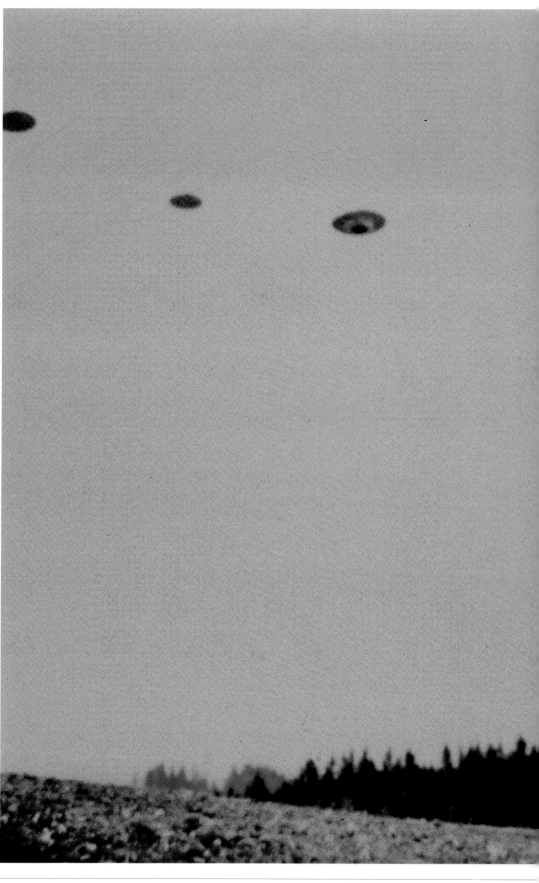

CHAPTER FIVE

CLOSE ENCOUNTERS OF THE FIFTH KIND

CLOSE ENCOUNTERS OF THE FIFTH KIND IMPLY A DIRECT contact or communication with an alien being or race. This contact can be either through telepathic means, or via the kind of abductions described in the previous chapter, but the most famous figures in this area, such as Billy Meier, claim to be able to communicate with ETs on a spiritual level.

As with other kinds of encounters with aliens, there is plenty of historical evidence to suggest that contact is not a modern day enigma – indeed, there may be proof of mankind's attempted communion with intelligent life from as far back as the Bible. This section will also deal with the particular mystery of the Nazca Lines in Peru, which, according to the celebrated German author Erich von Däniken, mark the site of an ancient airport. Could such sites prove that man has been forming an allegiance with aliens for centuries? Not only does von Däniken believe that our ancestors were in regular contact with alien visitors, who determined the course of ancient civilizations, but also that extraterrestrials may have tampered with our very genetic development.

An equally controversial subject when it comes to CE5s are crop circles. While several crop circle artists have come forward and admitted creating these shapes themselves, there are other circles for which there are no explanations, especially the most exotic and detailed. Some Ufologists and paranormal investigators argue that these intricate patterns are proof that humanity is being visited by highly evolved lifeforms, which are trying in vain to pass on a message for the future. A gallery of some of the most dramatic crop circles to appear in the UK is included. Many of the locations to bear crop circles are in recognized UFO hot spots, such as the English county of Wiltshire.

Finally, this chapter takes an in-depth look at mankind's attempts to make contact through such projects as SETI, or the Search for Extraterrestrial Intelligence, and CSETI, the Center for the Scientific Study of Extraterrestrial Intelligence. Instead of waiting for the aliens to find us, these organizations go out and attempt to initiate contact themselves. Hopefully, such organizations won't inadvertently attract the wrong kind of extraterrestrials, and subject Earth to a visit from a crew of intergalactic undesirables!

HISTORICAL ENCOUNTERS

- These shots were taken from a fresco carved around 6000 BC from Tassili in the Sahara Desert, Africa. These images are thought by some people to represent a space traveler, making contact with an ancient civilization.

THE EARLIEST EXAMPLES OF CLOSE Encounters of the Fifth Kind can be found in the Old Testament. The story concerns the Tower of Babel. God was angered at man's pride and vanity in trying to build a tower that stretched all the way to heaven, and prevented the builders from completing their goal. Instead, the tribes of man were scattered abroad and forced to speak in different tongues so humans could never again communicate in the same language.

Many Ufologists have claimed that the would-be builders of Babel were actually trying to build a tower to an alien spacecraft hovering above them. This hypothesis does make sense, especially given that they could never have hoped to

- Erich von Däniken, author of *Chariots of the Gods*, and other Ufology classics.

erect a tower which led straight up to the stars, and effectively out of the earth's atmosphere. So what were they aiming for? From the text it is apparent that the people could see something hovering in the sky, something which they believed to be heaven. Perhaps they were simply aiming their efforts toward a large mothership. Fully illuminated, this would have been a spectacular sight, and would have very much resembled a great floating city ...

THE NAZCA LINES
Further evidence of ancient alien encounters can be found in Peru, some Ufologists claim. Deep in the Nazcan desert is a mystery of awe-inspiring beauty – drawings of birds, animals, spiders,

clusters of stars and over 13,000 perfectly straight lines adorn the desert floor. Although the lines can be dated as far back as Stonehenge, they weren't discovered until 1927 when a Peruvian aerial survey team flew over the desert – despite their enormity and visual beauty, the carvings can only be viewed from above. A highway was built directly through them without anybody being aware of their existence.

All that can be seen from the ground are small narrow gullies, where the surface has been scrapped off to reveal the yellow earth hidden below. Many theories have been put forward to explain theses strange patterns. Erich von Däniken suggested that the lines were intricate runways, designed to guide in alien spacecraft, and enable them to land safely. However, many people believe this to be a little far-fetched, especially as most proponents of Ufology feel that alien craft land and take off vertically, and would therefore not need any guidance system,

ALIEN CRAFT LAND AND TAKE OFF VERTICALLY, AND WOULD THEREFORE NOT NEED ANY GUIDANCE SYSTEM, UNLESS OF COURSE, EVEN ALIEN TECHNOLOGY OF THOUSANDS OF YEARS AGO DID NOT ALLOW FOR VERTICAL TAKE OFF

unless of course, even alien technology of thousands of years ago did not allow for vertical take off (presumably aliens have had to evolve along with the rest of us!). It wasn't long before scientists and archaeologists were trying to piece together the two main puzzles: why and how the Nazca Lines were created. The answer to the second question was soon discovered by German astronomer Maria Reiche.

When Reiche first arrived at Nazca, at the start of a 40-year study of the lines, she was informed by the locals that within living memory, they could recall that wooden posts had been erected at intervals along the lines. This information acted as a catalyst to Reiche who firmly believed that the Nazcans had constructed the lines and the huge carvings, following a detailed plan. Reiche went on to claim that the constructions were created using, at first, small-scale models, which were later transposed onto the plains at Nazca. It has been estimated that the Nazcan dynasty began in 400BC and ended in 600AD, and during this time the Nazcan people became very adept and versatile, which is reflected in their pottery and ceramics. However, this does not account for their preoccupation with strange deities. When the lines were first drawn and the intricate figures of humming birds, spiders and even whales were etched out

• Maria Reiche (left) has spent most of her life investigating the Nazca Lines. Unlike Erich von Däniken, she doubts they were made by aliens.

• The Gateway of Sun in Tiwanaku, Bolivia. The edges are perfectly formed, as if carved with modern technology. It's roughly contemporary with the Nazca Lines.

- The El Castillo pyramid, located in Chichen Itza, Mexico – right in the heart of a notorious UFO hot spot. Believers in the ancient astronaut theory question how the ancient civilization responsible for this edifice could create such amazing symmetry.

- The dramatic Nazca Lines are eerily reminiscent of some kind of runway, perhaps for alien craft.

IF THE NAZCANS REALLY WERE IN CONTACT WITH ALIEN VISITORS WHAT BETTER WAY TO WARN THEM OFF THAN TO RECREATE AN ARMY OF GIGANTIC CREATURES ON THE DESERT SURFACE, AS A DETERRENT

of the desert surface, the Nazcans also simultaneously expressed themselves in their ceramics. Yet they suddenly began to create much stranger figures. The hillsides and some of the desert floor are adorned by "crowned men." These figures remain unexplained to this day, although many researchers have speculated that this was simply the Nazcan way of celebrating their gods. Erich von Däniken suggested in *Chariots of the Gods* that the lines at Nazca were in fact landing signals for extraterrestrial travelers, who presumably the Nazcans had mistaken as deities. Supposedly, the spacecraft would see the lines and patterns below and would therefore know where to land. Yet this theory does have its flaws, the most notable being that the physical make-up of the desert regions in Nazca are not in the slightest conducive to landing a spaceship – in fact if attempted, the craft would most probably become embedded, or at the very worst would topple over and crash.

However, von Däniken's theory can be turned on its head to create a completely new explanation. It is a well known fact that many countries have their countryside littered with hillside carvings, the Cerne Abbas Giant, in Dorset, England, being a prime example (as with the Nazcan Lines, we have no idea why the Cerne Abbas Giant was carved). Other researchers have suggested that these carvings were placed

- The Candelabra/Trident, located at Paracas, Peru. Ancient gods were frequently depicted holding tridents: natives believed the gods could use these tridents to alter meteorological conditions or summon thunder and lightning.

strategically in order to warn off any hostile warring tribes, after all, the sight from a distance of an enormous man brandishing an extremely large club, as is the case of the Cerne Abbas Giant, would be enough to terrify any invading army.

So if the Nazcans really were in contact with alien visitors, and they found their interference entirely unwelcome, what better way to warn them off than to recreate an army of gigantic creatures on the desert surface, as a deterrent. If the Nazcans knew that the beings arrived in strange spacecraft, which landed

vertically, they would have also known that the beings would be watching below during a landing in case of an accident, and what they would have seen was an array of huge birds and deadly spiders, enough to make even the most advanced civilizations think again about attempting to make contact. If this is the case, then this new theory may go some way to explaining the existence of the "crowned men" on the hillsides. The only thing that cannot be understood, is just how the Nazcans became airborne in the first place to have seen their handy work after it had been completed, and this piece of the puzzle may never be solved.

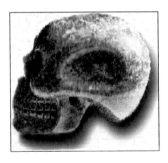

- One of the "crowned" men that appear on the hillsides surrounding the Nazca desert (left). Von Däniken believes these are representations of astronauts, who also left behind huge stones of peculiar composition (right).

- Both the Uffington White Horse in the English county of Oxfordshire, and the phallic Cerne Abbas Giant in the county of Dorset, are mysterious hill carvings that have never been adequately explained by historians and archaeologists. So strange are the figures that some scholars have suggested that they are crude representations of aliens who visited Britain thousands of years before Christ, carved by local tribes.

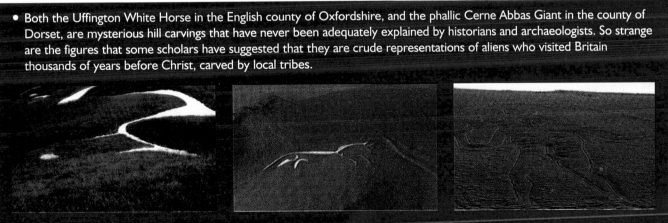

MODERN DAY CONTACTEES

AMONG THE MOST WELL KNOWN OF ALL alien contactees is George Adamski (above left), who claims to be the first man on the planet to have made one-to-one contact with races from outer space.

Flying Saucers Have Landed
Desmond Leslie & George Adamski

• Whether the work of a charlatan or not, Adamski's writing continues to influence.

Adamski's tale starts in California where he was practicing as a teacher of oriental philosophy and where, in 1940, he founded his own religious group, the Royal Order of Tibet before moving to Mount Palomar. In 1946, Adamski wrote a novel, which was unpublished, about an imaginary journey to Mars and Venus, followed up with another book in 1953 entitled *Flying Saucers Have Landed,* which he co-wrote with Desmond Leslie. This time the tale was strictly

non-fictional, and referred to his meetings with beings from other worlds. Adamski claimed that he and a group of friends had encountered a gigantic spacecraft near Desert Center, California. Adamski approached the object and met up with a male being whom he conversed with telepathically and by using sign language. This being was from the planet Venus, and had come to pass on knowledge that the citizens of the earth were destroying the atmosphere with their constant testing of atomic weaponry, and that since this testing was having an effect on other planets in the solar system, it must stop.

After this discussion Adamski was apparently taken on a tour of the spacecraft, and just before the craft took off again he had the opportunity to take a number of photographs – unfortunately only one of these was ever developed, and this was particularly blurred. Adamski was soon claiming that he was

• Adamski, who would pose as an astronomer, took numerous photos of UFOs, such as this cigar-shaped craft.

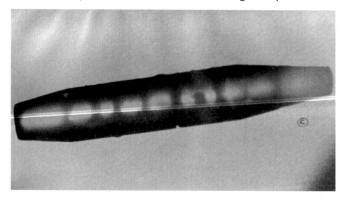

THIS BEING WAS FROM THE PLANET

VENUS, AND HAD COME TO PASS ON

KNOWLEDGE THAT THE CITIZENS OF

THE EARTH WERE DESTROYING THE

ATMOSPHERE WITH THEIR

CONSTANT TESTING OF ATOMIC

WEAPONRY

taken on numerous journeys in this vast spaceship to other planets, including Venus and Mars. He even claimed to have had sexual intercourse with beautiful Venusian women.

Adamski became a cult figure, and his writings inspired similar books from many other authors

ADAMSKI'S OUTLANDISH CLAIMS

Even though George Adamski made some outlandish claims, none could be more ridiculous than the case of the plaster-cast footprint. As evidence of his first encounter in the desert with Venusian beings, Adamski produced a plaster-cast footprint of the man whom he spoke with during the first meetings. The media came to question his credibility, however, when he was unable to explain why a party of friends out for a walk in the desert would be carrying a tub of plaster of Paris in the first place. It is thought that from this moment on Adamski was never going to be taken seriously, and he must have decided then that he may as well make his stories as outrageous as he wanted.

• These are two of the most famous photographs that Adamski took of what he claimed to be Venusian spacecraft. He claimed the top craft was a mothership that dispatched smaller scout craft.

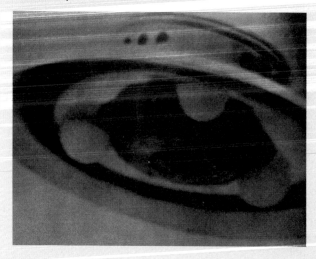

GREGORY'S HYBRID ENCOUNTER

In June 1994, Gregory had another vision. He was on board an alien scout craft, where he claims he met with a young psychic hybrid female whom he called Oona. Gregory is still in contact with Oona, and firmly believes that their relationship is leading to a higher understanding. He describes Oona as 23 years old and was born on Earth as a direct result of alien genetic engineering in the early 1970s. Oona has spent her entire life at a secret alien base in Russia and has never seen her home world. Her height is described as 4 feet 6 inches, and she is said to be slender with a slightly disproportionate head. She has big, dark, almond-shaped eyes, and her complexion is white with a slight pink tint. Her ears are small and child-like, as are her hands and feet.

When Gregory first noticed Oona on the scout ship, he felt a strange spirituality about her, which was validated when she turned and smiled at him. At last he realized that he was not an unwelcome intruder aboard the ship, he could be seen, and he could communicate telepathically with the hybrid female, as he has done on several occasions since.

• Adamski and modern day abductee Whitley Streiber were science fiction writers before claiming contact with UFOs, prompting skeptics to accuse them of mixing fact with fiction.

including Daniel Fry. Skeptics claim that he is a con artist, who dreamed up the alien encounter in order to revive his flagging career as a writer – his claims of contact with aliens were suspiciously similar to episodes described in his first fictional book.

THE PETER GREGORY ENCOUNTER

One of the most startling claims of contact with alien life forms comes from a well-respected psychic, living in England. Peter Gregory was no stranger to bizarre happenings, especially as his gift of psychic ability had opened his mind to many possibilities, but despite all his experience he was still astounded by what unfolded.

Before Gregory's alien contact began, there had been a lot of psychic phenomena and electrical interference in his home. Radios turned themselves

• An artist's impression of the ball of light Gregory saw prior to being abducted.

on and off, dark figures were noticed on the stairs by Gregory's wife, and the television would change channels of its own accord. Perhaps the most dramatic incident was when two glasses exploded with such a force that shards were blown 15 feet from the kitchen into the living room. In fact, the shards were so fine that the area looked as if it was covered by a fine layer of dust. The glasses had been stood on top of a cabinet, and upon examination resembled objects which had been exposed to extreme heat, as their bases were fused together.

Gregory's first encounter with a UFO was on 17th April 1993. He'd risen from bed at 2:30 am to go to the bathroom, when his attention was drawn to a light outside the landing window. He peered out and

TWO GLASSES EXPLODED WITH SUCH A FORCE THAT GLASS WAS BLOWN 15 FEET FROM THE KITCHEN INTO THE LIVING ROOM

saw a glowing ball of light, the size of a football. Gregory observed the phenomenon for about five seconds before it flew silently past the window and out of sight. After returning to bed Gregory felt a burning sensation in his temple, followed by an intense headache. He eventually fell into a deep sleep, when all of a sudden he had a vision. He remembers opening his eyes only to be greeted by a most peculiar sight. Gregory found himself in what appeared to be a control room, in an enormous flying machine. He knew he was airborne because he could feel the movement beneath his feet, as if in an elevator. This motion was accompanied by a humming noise. Gregory noticed that the room was illuminated with an intense blue light, which seemed to pulse in an almost hypnotic state. He entered a state of deep inner euphoria, until without warning the light vanished, and he found himself on the floor of the spacecraft. The room was an oval shape, with a large console in the center. The console was about 10 feet in length, and fitted with a display of lights which flashed in sequence. On the left of the console was a cubicle which stood about 6 feet in height, and was illuminated. Gregory noticed, standing 15 feet from him, three humanoid figures staring at a viewing monitor watching a

• Peter Gregory's impression of the inside of the spacecraft where he was taken. Gregory claims he was shown both the past and present history of the planet Earth on the screen to the top left of the drawing. According to the aliens who abducted him, the only way mankind can survive a future cataclysm will be to retreat underground.

- Billy Meier claims that he was contacted by Semjase, a female extraterrestrial from the Pleiadian star system on 28th January 1975. This was the first in a series of over 100 contacts, some of which resulted in Meier being able to photograph Semjase's "beamship." The photos have become an integral part of UFO lore.

HE DESCRIBED THEM AS BEING ABOUT THE SAME SIZE AS HUMANS, WITH DEEP-BLUE PIERCING EYES, REDDISH-BROWN HAIR, AND HEADS CIRCLED BY A BROAD SILVER BAND WHICH APPEARED TO HAVE A STATIC LIGHT ON EITHER SIDE

transmission. The beings didn't seem to notice that Gregory was in the room; he described them as being about the same size as humans, with deep-blue piercing eyes, reddish-brown hair, and heads circled by a broad silver band which appeared to have a static light on either side. Gregory made his way closer towards them, and noticed an on-screen display which read "Year 3600." He realized that the on-screen display was showing the destruction of civilization, also indicating that man had to move below the earth's surface in order to survive.

This amazing event was only the beginning for Gregory, and soon he was somewhat of a celebrity in his home town. He has managed to capture minutes of UFO footage on video, which has been subjected to analysis and found to be faultless.

THE ASTOUNDING BILLY MEIER

The name Billy Meier has become synonymous with alien contact, making him one of the most talked about people in the field of Ufology.

Meier (above) was born in 1937, in Bulach, Switzerland and is now rumored to be living in a

- The Pleiadians agreed to let Meier photograph their beamships to support his story. On six of these pre-arranged flybys, Meier took along his super 8mm movie camera and obtained filmed footage of the beamships. Opinion is divided on the images' veracity, since the super 8mm films and the negatives have been conveniently "lost."

   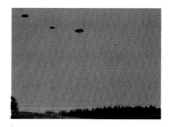

- When pushed for harder evidence, Meier stated that he had been given adequate proof by the Pleiadians but that he was not allowed to use it. Apparently the Pleiadians do not want to "violate the freedom of choice rule" – in other words, it is up to us whether we believe Meier's claims or not.

- This "wedding cake" photograph looks distinctly suspicious, but Meier claims it is genuine. It has been suggested that he faked some of the images of UFOs passing by trees. A computer-enhancement of one photograph reveals that the "UFO" itself was very small and had been placed in front of a (model?) tree. Other tests showed that Meier had used a miniature tree in locations where trees did not exist.

commune in that country with a number of his most ardent followers. Meier shot to fame in 1975 when he claimed to be in contact with an alien race from a star constellation known as the Pleiades. These beings apparently lived on a planet called Erra. One of the beings which Meier was in contact with became known as Semjase, a name which he invented in order to catch out anybody else claiming to be in contact with the same beings.

Over a period of approximately three years, Meier was able to amass a collection of some 12,000 clear, daylight photos of the Pleiadian scout crafts, motherships and beamships. Furthermore, he was taught about aspects of humanity by these beings – where we came from and where we are heading –

OVER A PERIOD OF APPROXIMATELY THREE YEARS, MEIER WAS ABLE TO AMASS A COLLECTION OF SOME 12,000 CLEAR, DAYLIGHT PHOTOS OF THE PLEIADIAN SCOUT CRAFTS, MOTHERSHIPS AND BEAMSHIPS

and claimed to be in contact with the Pleiadians on a weekly basis. Meier apparently recorded every meeting and all the information handed down to him, some of which included the methods used by the beings for space/time travel. Meier's documentation has never been published. In October 1978, the contacts ended, although Meier has maintained that he can still make contact telepathically.

One of the most amazing aspects of the Meier contacts is the astounding clarity of his photographs – photographs which the Pleiadians allowed, and indeed encouraged him to take.

Of course it has been rumored that the pictures are fakes, and that model spaceships were found on his farm, indicating a deception, but these rumors have never been substantiated. What is known, however, is that the photograph of "Asket," another one of his supposed spiritual guides, was actually taken in a Swedish modeling agency!

Yet interest in the Meier case remains high, and a movie is even being made about his remarkable life. Certainly, Meier has benefited from the publicity. He currently has several "mates" in addition to his wife and has reportedly had several children by them. The cult that has grown up around Meier has also brought him money and land, donated by acolytes.

TAKING THE INITIATIVE

WHILE MOST OF MANKIND'S contact with aliens seems to be involuntary, there exists a group of individuals who are attempting to take the initiative by instigating contact. They are known as the Center for the Study of Extraterrestrial Intelligence (CSETI) and are based in North Carolina.

CSETI was founded by Dr Steven Greer, and is a nonprofit organization, concerned primarily with research and educational study of extraterrestrials. More importantly, the association serves as a diplomatic organization attempting to establish open and friendly contact with any alien civilization visiting the earth. CSETI have evaluated that there are at least four differing races presently visiting this planet and that members of CSETI's field workers have come within close proximity to several types of spacecraft. They also estimate that the success rate of human-initiated contact, including the boarding of a spaceship by a highly trained team of researchers, is very high. CSETI has

about 25 working groups around the globe, consisting of trained individuals who are prepared to brave any conditions – not only to observe alien spacecraft, but to make contact. CSETI also boasts a senior team, known as the Rapid Mobilization and Investigative Team (RMIT). This team is used world-wide for establishing interactive contact with structured spacecraft, and their occupants.

The organization has had some staggering results. On one occasion, founder Steven Greer was invited to Gulf Breeze, Florida, the scene of multiple UFO sightings for some years now, in order to attempt to make contact. On the night of 14th March 1992, a group of nearly 40 people were based along the Gulf Breeze coastline. After a period of meditation, Steven Greer took some powerful flashlights from his bag

- A key part of CSETI is the Rapid Mobilization and Investigative Team (RMIT). This team is used world-wide for establishing interactive contact with structured spacecraft, and their occupants. Recently, for example, CSETI members were dispatched to Scotland to investigate a video recording of a strange craft obtained by an elderly couple in the UFO hot spot of Bonnybridge.

1950
WHITE SANDS, NEW MEXICO
BIG APPLE UFO TOUR
On 4th July, Daniel Fry, an employee at the White Sands proving ground, came into contact with an alien spacecraft and its occupants. Fry was at the V2 test site when the craft appeared above him. He was even taken on a quick trip in the object across New York and into space.

1952
MOJAVE DESERT, CALIFORNIA
ADAMSKI'S FIRST ENCOUNTER
On 20th November, budding science fiction writer George Adamski claimed to have made the first of several contacts with alien beings from Venus, in the Mojave Desert. The occupants of a cigar-shaped craft that met Adamski took him on the first of many journeys through the galaxy.

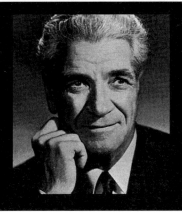

1954
LONDON, ENGLAND
VOICES FROM THE ETHER
One July day, George King had his first encounter with aliens from Venus whilst practicing yoga in his apartment. The voice in his head told him that he was to be the voice of the interplanetary parliament. King claimed to become a channeler of the aliens, and later formed a quasi-religious cult.

and began to make intricate patterns of triangles in the night sky. Greer soon became aware of the presence of UFOs and alerted the rest of the group to the fact that there would be more than one craft. No sooner had he spoken than three "typical" red UFOs appeared in the area of sky where Greer had been training his flashlights. He then took a more powerful light from his bag and began to flash sequences of lights to the objects, and on many occasions the objects responded with the same number of flashes. This was a true Close Encounter of the Fifth Kind, initiated by humans. Interestingly, the MUFON (Mutual UFO Network) report for that evening included statements from more than 50 witnesses of seven UFOs seen from seven different locations.

> GREER SOON BECAME AWARE OF THE
> PRESENCE OF UFOS AND ALERTED
> THE REST OF THE GROUP TO THE
> FACT THAT THERE WOULD BE MORE
> THAN ONE CRAFT

On another occasion, while in Belgium, a CSETI research group managed to make contact with a huge triangular extraterrestrial craft. The group apparently used telepathy to call the craft down from the clouds for a quick glimpse: the object was described as having a white light at each apex, and was completely soundless until it began to hover directly above them, at which point it started to emit an intense humming noise.

Yet CSETI's most spectacular contact took place in Mexico City on 1st February 1993. Due to the

• CSETI claims it held a group vigil in Gulf Breeze, Florida in 1993, and communicated with assembled UFOs via flashlight (celebrated in the above display). The same evening, another group called MUFON (Mutual UFO Network) reported that more than 50 witnesses had seen seven UFOs. Of course, it could just be coincidence ...

1954
MICHIGAN
ALIENS CALL BACK
Ham radio operator Richard Miller got more than he bargained for when aliens began responding to his messages. After arriving at an appointed meeting place, a staircase descended from a UFO and Miller was beckoned aboard. He was shown key events in man's history, including the Big Bang.

1956
ARLINGTON, VIRGINIA
PENTAGON MEETING
Dr Frank Strange claims to have met an alien from Venus called Val Thor in the Pentagon. The Venusian, who looked like a human but without fingerprints, told Strange that he was in the building with the consent of the US government, who were apparently testing his clothing.

1965
VENEZUELA
ORION EMISSARIES
On 7th August, three businessmen claimed to have encountered two very tall men, about 8 feet in height with long yellow hair and large eyes. The entities, who appeared within a beam of light emanating from a hovering UFO, claimed to have come in peace from the constellation of Orion.

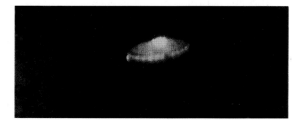

- CSETI continue to carry out their work in the hope that one day mankind will join as one in welcoming these visitors from space, and ultimately take heed of the messages they are bringing us.

increased activity in and around the Mexican capital, the group decided to attempt to make contact with aliens on 30th January 1993. That evening the team went out to an area around the volcanic zone, on the south side of the city, and climbed to an altitude of about 10,000 feet where they set up base camp. The group had been tempted to visit Mexico as a result of a sighting on 1st January that year, of silver disks floating over Mexico City, an event apparently witnessed by hundreds of thousands of people. Once the base camp was set up, the group set about routine testing of equipment, not expecting to make contact on the first night. However, during testing, a brilliant amber light approached them out of the northwest skies. The entire group was engulfed by an intense amber light, which seemed to have no source.

- UFOs over Mexico

CSETI decided that the next day they should go around to the other side of the mountain, because reports indicated that UFO activity was greater on that side, and the location was also more secure. The group settled into a hotel, and in the evening set out to hike to a site of high activity. At approximately 11:40 pm, whilst the entire group was practicing a visualization technique called "remote viewing," they became aware that a spacecraft was approaching.

Looking into the night sky they discovered a huge triangular-shaped spacecraft, seemingly circling as though searching for the group. They began to signal to the craft with the high-powered lights, and the craft instantly began to move towards them. All the time members of CSETI were remote viewing the pilot of the craft, whilst the rest of the group

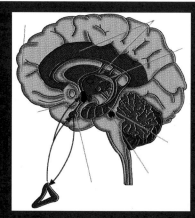

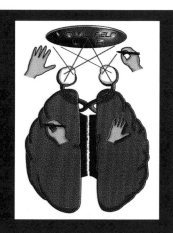

- In remote viewing, a visualization technique practiced by CSETI, the stressors in the front of the brain are shut down in order to cultivate psychic ability. Tim Rifat (left) of the UK is an expert remote viewer.

continued to make contact with the light beams. Attempts were made to photograph this event but at the crucial moment all electronic equipment failed – although it functioned perfectly well before and after the episode. The group continued to signal to the craft, and it appeared to be responding, and then it began to descend as if landing. As it did this, a smaller scout craft emerged from the mothership, but as soon as fresh camera equipment was brought out the craft stopped, the larger ship then made a 360° turn and they both left.

The group maintained contact with alien crafts for the following couple of days, and although they have no photographic evidence of their encounters, the case is fully documented and classified as a genuine Close Encounter of the Fifth Kind. CSETI continue to carry out their work in the hope that one day mankind will join as one in welcoming these visitors from space, and ultimately take heed of the messages they are bringing us.

A SMALLER SCOUT CRAFT EMERGED

FROM THE MOTHERSHIP, BUT AS

SOON AS FRESH CAMERA

EQUIPMENT WAS BROUGHT OUT THE

CRAFT STOPPED, THE LARGER SHIP

THEN MADE A 360° TURN AND THEY

BOTH LEFT

THE SEARCH FOR EXTRATERRESTRIAL INTELLIGENCE

In January 1996, a culmination of staggering events resulted in the discovery of three new planets in the constellation of Virgo, and SETI (Search for Extraterrestrial Intelligence), acting on the find, received an organized pulse from that region of space. However, these events went almost unnoticed by the world's media – quite unbelievable considering the far-reaching implications.

Geoffrey Marcy and Paul Butler, two US astronomers who had instigated a program of collating data from the Lick Observatory in California, made some even more startling discoveries. They unwittingly discovered two new planets at first, and then they found a third enormous planet, nine times the mass of Jupiter, which they named HD 114762. The planets had odd

SIGNALS FROM SPACE

Taking a radically different approach to CSETI is the similarly named SETI (Search for Extraterrestrial Intelligence). Originally set up by independent scientific organizations and astronomical societies, and enjoying the early patronage of eminent scientists such as the late Carl Sagan, SETI use a barrage of radio telescopes and other equipment to scour the universe in the hope of picking up any kind of message that would suggest intelligent life. So far, SETI have been unable to pinpoint any evidence, although the project is proving worthwhile for its ability to detect new astronomical phenomena. The problem behind SETI's approach is that they assume an alien civilization would be able to understand our message even if they could receive it. Owing to the huge distances in space, aliens would only just be receiving messages sent out by the predecessors of SETI some 30 years ago. There have also been some memorable false alarms: on 20th January 1996, astronomers at Parkes Observatory in Australia picked up a faint radio signal every evening. It turned out to be coming from a microwave in a downstairs office ...

• Crop circles, such as this one in the county of Wiltshire, have become a common sight on the English landscape.

• The cruder circles suggest humans are responsible, working secretly – with a risk of criminal prosecution – at night.

THE CIVILIZATION THAT BLURTS OUT ITS EXISTENCE ON INTERSTELLAR BEACONS AT THE FIRST OPPORTUNITY MAY BE LIKE SOME HOMINID DESCENDING FROM THE TREES CALLING 'HERE KITTY!' TO SOME SABRE TOOTH TIGER

egg-shaped orbits around the star Virginis 70 in the constellation of Virgo. The astronomers made their momentous findings using a technique known as the Döppler effect. This works by measuring the wobble of a star which is caused by the gravitational forces of orbiting objects. After their discovery, Marcy was

even hesitant in using the term "planet" due to the immense size of the find. This inspirational discovery was the catalyst for SETI to investigate the newly found solar system. They sent a pulse into the region using their advanced radar technology and received what appeared to be an organized and repetitive signal. The signal was first heard by scientists working on the Serendip 3 project for SETI. A further concentrated search of this region of space took place in early 1997; the results so far are inconclusive. Despite the sheer enormity of the find, scientists are remaining skeptical, especially in the light of some previous finds which turned out to be entirely terrestrial. But they would be drawn to suggest that this signal is "highly unusual" and the possibility remains that this could be ET-related.

Despite SETI's apparent good work, they have also attracted their fair share of critics. Professor Robert

1990

ARGENTINA
SOUTHERN SEARCH
On Columbus Day, Argentinian astronomers were finally given the go head to start the first search of the galaxies conducted in the Southern Hemisphere. They constructed two 98-feet dishes in order to receive and send signals into the center of the Milky Way. There have been no replies yet.

1996

USA
PLANETARY SYSTEM DISCOVERED
On July 13th 1996, a new planetary system was announced by astronomers, located around the star Lalande 21185. Lalande is the fourth closest star to us, being just over eight light years away from the sun. Early indications suggest the system would be unable to support life – as we know it.

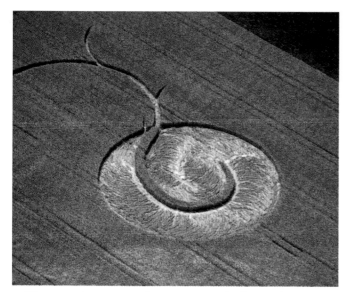

• The more intricate circles continue to baffle, as it's unlikely they could be completed in one evening.

• Even more strangely, some crop circle artists have reported strange lights and paranormal phenomena while working.

Road of Harvard University, questions the wisdom of beaming signals into space out of concern that we might attract some extraterrestrial undesirables: "The civilization that blurts out its existence on interstellar beacons at the first opportunity may be like some hominid descending from the trees calling 'here kitty!' to some sabre tooth tiger."

THE MESSAGE IS CLEAR
The phenomenon which many people point to as positive proof of contact by alien beings with humanity is that of crop circles.

Crop circle researchers have always believed that UFOs may be responsible for those

formations that are obviously not the work of man, but why aliens would create such phenomena has never been adequately explained. Of course, many alternative theories have been put forward for the creation of these beautiful formations, including tiny whirlwinds and even insect infestation, but most people return to the more fanciful belief that the occupants of alien spacecraft are the real perpetrators of the circles.

Is it possible, therefore, that alien races have been visiting this planet for centuries, leaving behind messages fashioned in corn fields. In fact, 1996 saw some of the most impressive crop circles ever to appear in England, or for that

1996
ANTARCTICA
MARTIAN LIFE FINALLY FOUND?
On 11th August 1996, NASA scrutinized a melon-sized meteorite uncovered in Antarctica in 1984 and announced it contained a fossil of a long-extinct life form. Although the life form was only a single celled organism, it was still proof that life did exist on Mars billions of years ago.

1996
STONEHENGE, ENGLAND
HUGE CROP CIRCLE APPEARS
One of the largest and most impressive crop formations ever to appear in the British Isles was discovered on 7th July 1996. The formation, in a field adjacent to the ancient British monument of Stonehenge, was rumored by farmers to have appeared in just 30 minutes.

• Silbury Hill, Wiltshire: barley crop.

• Olivers Castle, Wiltshire: wheat crop.

matter Europe. Most of these formations exhibited a level of detail virtually impossible to recreate. The following is a selection of the 12 most beautiful and awe-inspiring of the 1996 crop, together with a brief description of where they appeared and the crop in which they were found. Enjoy their beauty and decide for yourselves, are extraterrestrials trying to tell us something, which we are too ignorant at this stage to understand?

MOST PEOPLE RETURN TO THE MORE

FANCIFUL BELIEF THAT THE

OCCUPANTS OF ALIEN SPACECRAFT

ARE THE REAL PERPETRATORS OF

THE CIRCLES

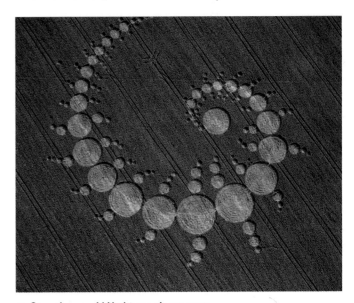

• Stonehenge, Wiltshire: wheat crop.

• Liddington, Wiltshire: wheat crop.

• Little Bury Green, Essex: barley crop.

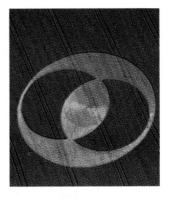

• Ashbury, Oxfordshire: wheat crop.

• Alton Barnes, Wiltshire: barley crop.

• Iddington, Wiltshire: wheat crop.

• Goodworth, Hampshire: barley crop.

• Barton le Clay,
Bedfordshire: wheat crop.

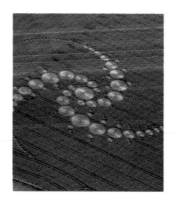

• Windmill Hill, Wiltshire:
wheat crop.

CROP HOAXERS

Back in 1991, two British men called Doug Bower and Dave Chorley claimed that they had invented crop circles in 1978, and had made most of the circles since that time. The numerous inconsistencies in their story suggest that while the pair were probably involved to an extent, they could have only managed the simpler formations. A more credible pair were British photographer Rob Irving and Jim Schnabel, an American resident in the UK. They crafted many formations in 1992 and 1993 and although this confused researchers, Irving and Schnabel said their hoaxing was another form of research. It helped them to see how circles were made and how easy it was to fool people. Another pair of crop circle artists, John Lundberg and Rod Dickinson, have reported numerous instances of strange lights and UFOs, as well as a sense of dark foreboding while at work.

CHAPTER SIX

HOT SPOTS
OF THE
WORLD

IF A PARTICULAR LOCALITY HAS MORE THAN ITS FAIR SHARE of UFO activity then it is known as a UFO "hot spot." However, this doesn't mean that the location will always be a place where the skywatcher is guaranteed a glimpse of a flying saucer. Even though there may have been numerous accounts of UFOs in a certain area, this won't ensure that sightings will continue to be recorded.

One probable explanation for why some locations seem more prone to UFO activity than others, is increased public awareness of what constitutes a UFO in the first place. The developed world, where most hot spots are found, tends to be more densely populated than certain other territories (some areas of the African continent, for example) and the locals are more aware of what is going on in the skies above them. Also, skywatchers in the developed world are probably more aware of what does and does not belong up there, while some inhabitants of remoter, less technologically developed areas, may have problems determining the differences between an airplane and an Unidentified Flying Object.

The most famous hot spots have become the meccas of Ufology – places such as Gulf Breeze, Florida, Warminster and Bonnybridge in the UK, and Mexico City, will be familiar to anyone with a passing interest in the subject. Indeed, Mexico City continues to yield an astonishing number of UFO sightings.

The following anecdote gives an idea of the regularity with which strange craft are reported. Following one of the celebrated UFO "fly-bys" on Mexican Independence Day, 1993 (see Chapter Two), a TV program called *Frenie al Publico* debated the UFO phenomenon in a live broadcast. The host of the program speculated that UFOs were monitoring the airwaves and sent an open invitation to the visitors to reveal themselves to the viewers before the end of the show. As the show came to a close, two UFOs, in the guise of strange materializing lights suspended in the air, appeared nearby. Mexico's UFOs also seem to be very active around volcanoes, which that country has in abundance. Some 80% of sightings in central Mexico have been reported in the vicinity of a volcano, and Mexican Ufologists have speculated that the UFOs regularly spotted around Mt Popcateptepl in Puebla were warning of the volcano's imminent eruption, which took place in December 1994.

The evidence of the last 50 years suggests that a large number of UFOs continue to be seen. Where they come from is an entirely different matter…

NORTH AMERICA

USA

WHERE: Area 51, Nevada
WHEN: Numerous occasions

1 The secret military complex that some Ufologists believe lies within the huge Nellis Range has been host to many UFO sightings, perhaps confirming the theory that the heavily guarded base conceals captured alien spacecraft. The nearest town, Rachel, records most of the sightings, but UFOs have been spotted as far afield as Las Vegas.

WHERE: Washington DC
WHEN: 19-20th July 1952

2 UFOs were sighted by many people, civilians and military personnel alike, flying over the nation's capital. Further sightings in the Washington area were reported on 26th July.

Photographs taken of the objects appeared in the national newspapers the following day, although the official statement from the USAF was that the objects were actually "temperature inversions."

WHERE: Gulf Breeze, Florida
WHEN: 21st May 1996

3 Two black triangular UFOs were sighted over the beach. The same two UFOs were seen again, further north, the following day. Gulf Breeze has been a hot spot for UFO sightings for many years, and has produced some intriguing pictures, as well as the attentions of research groups such as CSETI.

MEXICO

WHERE: Mexico City
WHEN: 11th July 1991

4 A solar eclipse was overshadowed by the appearance of a metallic saucer. Mass UFO sightings have been reported every Mexican Independence Day (16th September) since 1991.

WEST INDIES

WHERE: Puerto Rico
WHEN: 28th April 1992

5 A saucer-like object pursued by an F-14 Tomcat was sighted by a man repairing his truck. Eventually, the UFO split into two pieces, with each part heading in a different direction.

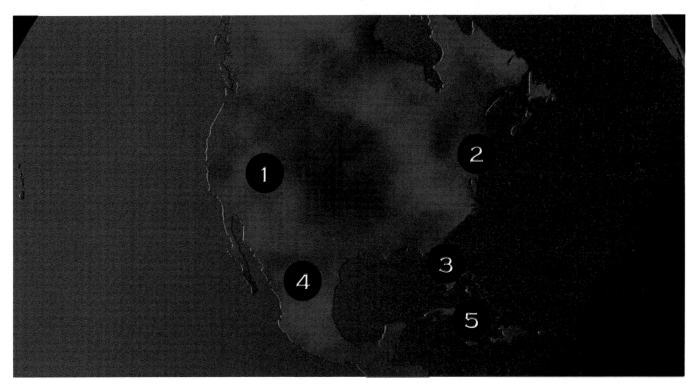

SOUTH AMERICA

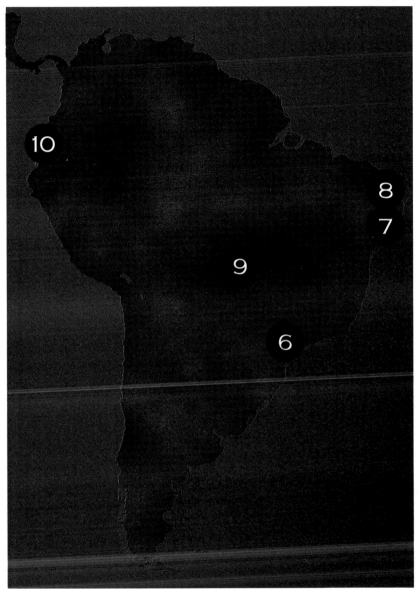

WHERE: Joao Pessoa
WHEN: 16th October 1996

7 A giant rectangular UFO was spotted by many witnesses over Northern Brazil, which was described as being "as long as a 20-storey building." It was also seen in ten other cities in the surrounding area, causing over 300 people to flee in panic.

WHERE: Campina Grande
WHEN: 17th October 1996

8 A triangular-shaped UFO was witnessed by diners in an eleventh floor restaurant as it glided over the town of Campina Grande.

Back in nearby Joao Pessoa, UFOs were witnessed flying in formation over the town. One eye-witness, a professor, counted 11 UFOs during the second pass and 30 during the third. Again, the Brazilian Air Force refused to verify a UFO sighting.

WHERE: Pilozinhas
WHEN: 18th October 1996

9 A 92-year-old witness claimed that "an unusual silver plane" landed on her farm during the early evening. "Little fantastic men" emerged from the craft and proceeded to communicate with the woman in a high-pitched unintelligible language. Since language proved to be rather a barrier, the strange men stole some of the woman's chickens and promptly left.

BRAZIL

WHERE: Varghina
WHEN: 20th January 1996

6 A UFO sighting at daybreak may be connected to the alleged survival of its extraterrestrial occupants. Three young girls claimed to have seen a small, brown-skinned creature squatting in a pathway. Although the military authorities deny that anything out of the ordinary happened, there are rumors of a farmhand killing one of the beings with his shotgun.

ECUADOR

WHERE: Salinas, Ecuador
WHEN: June 1996

10 A UFO was witnessed by 30 police officers, over the Salinas Art Academy on the Pacific coast of Ecuador. The object, which was not picked up on radar, hovered at around 900 feet for two hours before disappearing across the bay.

EUROPE

BELGIUM

WHERE: Eupen
WHEN: 29th November 1989

1 A UFO was sighted in the early evening by two Sergeant-Majors of the Belgian *gendarmerie*. The craft, traveling slowly above a field, was described as a triangular-shaped platform of up to 200 feet wide. The UFO had three light-projecting beams and emitted a low humming noise. The Belgian Air Force had detected the object on radar and an aircraft was dispatched to follow the craft until it disappeared.

WHERE: Liège
WHEN: 15th December 1989

2 The Belgian Air Force attempted to intercept a series of UFOs, but with no success.

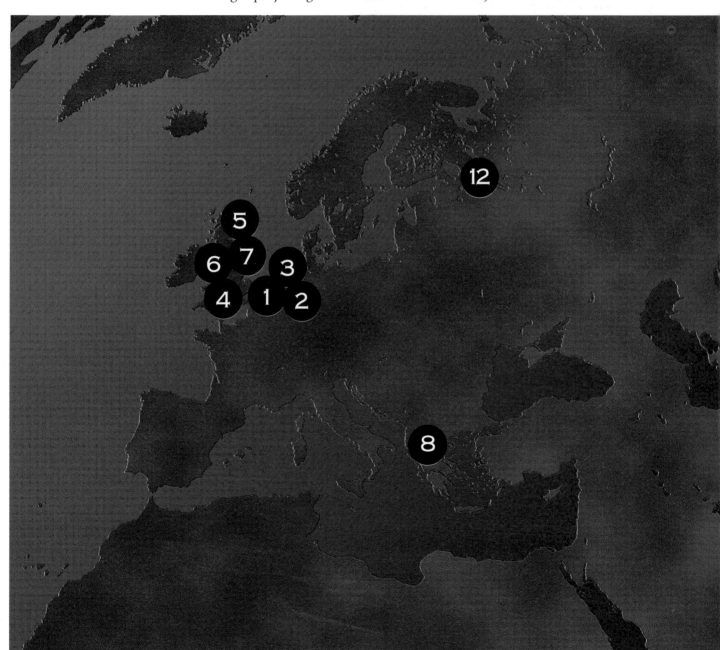

WHERE: Wavre, Tubize and Brussels
WHEN: 30-31st March 1990

3 The Belgian *gendarmerie* received many reports from the public of UFOs in the skies over Wavre, 12 miles south of Brussels. The UFO appeared to be the same triangular object sighted in Eupen the previous November.

Two Belgian F-16 fighter aircraft were dispatched by the air force, who confirmed interception of a triangular object. The fighter craft pursued the "wildly erratic" object for an hour before they lost it – there was no way the Belgian pilots could match the seemingly impossible speeds achieved by the UFOs.

Following this incident, the Belgian authorities were inundated with over 13,500 witnesses to the "flying triangle," 2,500 of which provided written reports.

GREAT BRITAIN

WHERE: Warminster, Wiltshire
WHEN: February 1965

4 The market town of Warminster has been reporting UFOs since the 1950s. One of the strangest incidents took place in 1965, when a sonic wave was heard over the country house of the Marquess of Bath. A flock of pigeons flew into the high-pitched vibrating hum, and each bird dropped to the ground, dead. Warminster declared itself to be the official UFO capital of Great Britain on 28th October 1996.

WHERE: Bonnybridge, Scotland
WHEN: 27th October 1992

5 A family traveling by car reported seeing a black UFO with strange green lights above this Scottish town. This was the start of a series of unexplained UFO sightings which continue with intermittent frequency. To date, over 2,000 UFO and strange aerial phenomena have been reported above the town.

UFOs were photographed and captured on videotape resulting in an intense media interest from as far afield as the US and Japan. A copy of a videotape of the most recent sighting was recently taken back to the US for further investigation by the UFO research group CSETI, sparking a row over accusations that they'd managed to obtained the original.

WHERE: Keighley, Yorkshire
WHEN: 27th December 1995

6 Large metallic objects were seen hovering in the skies above this northern county before the craft apparently changed its shape.

WHERE: Scammonden, Yorkshire
WHEN: 28th March 1996

7 Orange balls of light were seen around the Scammonden area, a major local hot spot. On one occasion the object appeared to be writing symbols in the sky before it changed shape into a triangle and disappeared without trace.

GREECE

WHERE: Megas Platanos
WHEN: 2nd September 1990

8 Villagers claimed to observe a small group of five to six UFOs coming towards them, one of which crashed into the ground. During the rest of that night the other UFOs apparently collected the remains of the destroyed ship. Furthermore, the villagers claimed to have salvaged some fragments of the crashed craft.

FORMER USSR

WHERE: Unknown locations
WHEN: 21st March 1990

9 Over 100 UFO observations reported to the Chief of Staff of the former USSR's Air Defense Forces.

WHERE: Turkmenistan
WHEN: 25th May 1990

10 Two jet fighters intercepted a UFO hovering over a nearby town. Both planes were repelled by the UFO and crashed, killing the occupants.

WHERE: Frunze
WHEN: 21st September 1990

11 UFO sighting and subsequent landing witnessed by three members of the Russian military.

WHERE: St Petersburg
WHEN: 2nd March 1991

12 Numerous triangular-shaped UFO were picked up on radar over the city. When a squadron of local fighter aircraft were dispatched to intercept the craft, nothing was found.

AUSTRALIA

WHERE: Queensland
WHEN: 19th January 1966

1 A farmer saw a strange machine rise from a nearby swamp, emitting a loud hissing noise. The blue-gray spinning object rose to around 60 feet above the farmer before moving away at a terrific speed.

Investigations into the area brought to light similar sightings of the object by other people in the area, preceding the farmer's encounter. The story made the front page of the Sydney *Sun-Herald.*

WHERE: Nemingha, New South Wales
WHEN: 22nd March 1976

2 Just before dawn, a couple driving to the town of Murrundi stopped to consult the map. A small white car approached them and they tried to flag it down in the hope the occupants could give them directions. Suddenly, a bright yellow-green light appeared from above, obscuring the car. The car moved over to the wrong side of the road, before being totally enveloped in a whitish haze. A woman got out of the car and wiped what appeared to be a white substance off her windshield. When the cloth

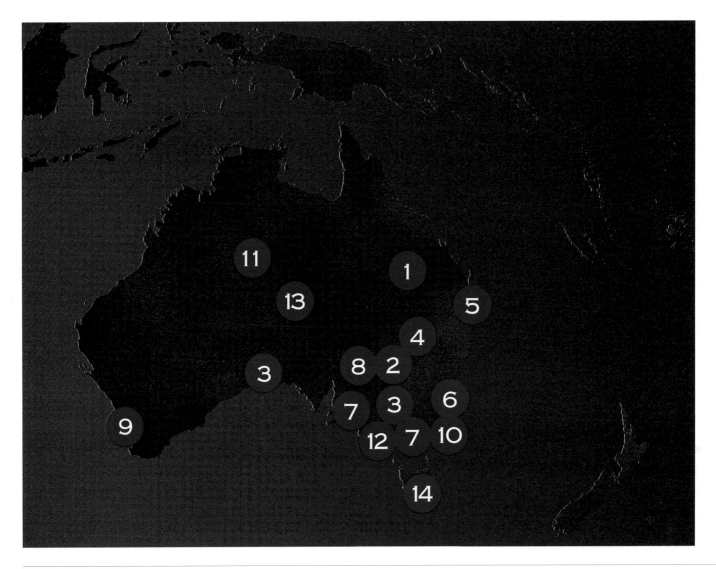

hit the ground, it burst into flames. The woman drove off, oblivious to the couple's presence. This is believed to be one of the few UFO incidents reported only by third-party witnesses.

WHERE: Victoria
WHEN: 30th September 1980

3 A cattle rancher witnessed a large domed disk floating several feet above the ground just outside his home. The object landed at first 50 feet away, but quickly rose with an "ear-splitting" whine when approached, before flying away.

A ring of blackened grass was left where the flying saucer had landed. Even more strangely, the rancher went on to claim that his water tank, which the saucer had flown over, had been mysteriously drained of its contents.

WHERE: Coonabarabran
WHEN: 15th November 1994

4 Six people reported sightings of a UFO around 9:00 pm in the Coonabarabran area. According to local police reports, witnesses saw bright lights directly across a roadway and also noticed a large diamond-shaped object hovering silently above a house. The eye-witnesses reported hearing a loud roaring noise as the object sped off.

WHERE: Brisbane
WHEN: 28th April 1995

5 An egg-shaped UFO giving out an orange light was seen by almost a dozen people, a few days after a similar craft was reported in the cities of Adelaide and Melbourne. Eye-witnesses claim that the object traveled across the sky before disappearing in a series of dots.

WHERE: Darwin
WHEN: 4th February 1996

6 A bright orange UFO was witnessed by 14 people as they were having a barbecue in the Darwin suburb of Jingili.

WHERE: Adelaide, Sydney and Melbourne
WHEN: 14-16th June 1996

7 Strange orange balls of light were sighted over three major Australian cities. The national television network, TENTV, showed video footage of a bright orange UFO, which many Ufologists believe was the same craft reported in Brisbane on 28th April the previous year.

WHERE: Chelsea-Frankston, Victoria
WHEN: 23rd June 1996

8 There were numerous UFO sightings in the Chelsea-Frankston area of Victoria.

The Australian UFO Hotline was to receive more than 20 calls from people claiming to have seen five orange lights moving in formation at around midnight.

WHERE: Perth
WHEN: 21st August 1996

9 A cigar-shaped object was reported by over 100 people. The object traveled overhead, causing chaos on the roads during the city's rush hour.

WHERE: Canberra
WHEN: 21st August 1996

10 Balls of blue and white light were seen moving across the sky, before departing at great speed.

WHERE: Packenham
WHEN: 22nd August 1996

11 Large yellow and orange lights were seen traveling overhead, stopping for a short period of time before heading off at speed.

WHERE: Melbourne
WHEN: 21st September 1996

12 A large bluish-white object, at first believed to have been a meteor, was reported over Melbourne. Witnesses described the object as being two disks, one on top of the other, with a collection of colored lights in the center.

WHERE: Pine Gap
WHEN: Numerous occasions

13 This US-owned communications base has seen frequent UFO activity in recent years. It has been speculated that the overseas base serves a similar function to Area 51.

WHERE: Tasmania
WHEN: 3rd November 1996

14 UFOs described by witnesses as "space blobs" were sighted over the Tasmanian town of Kempton. The following morning, residents were surprised to discover blobs of white transparent jelly littering the streets. The substance was examined by Australia's National UFO Reporting Centre and was found to contain micro-organisms.

ASIA

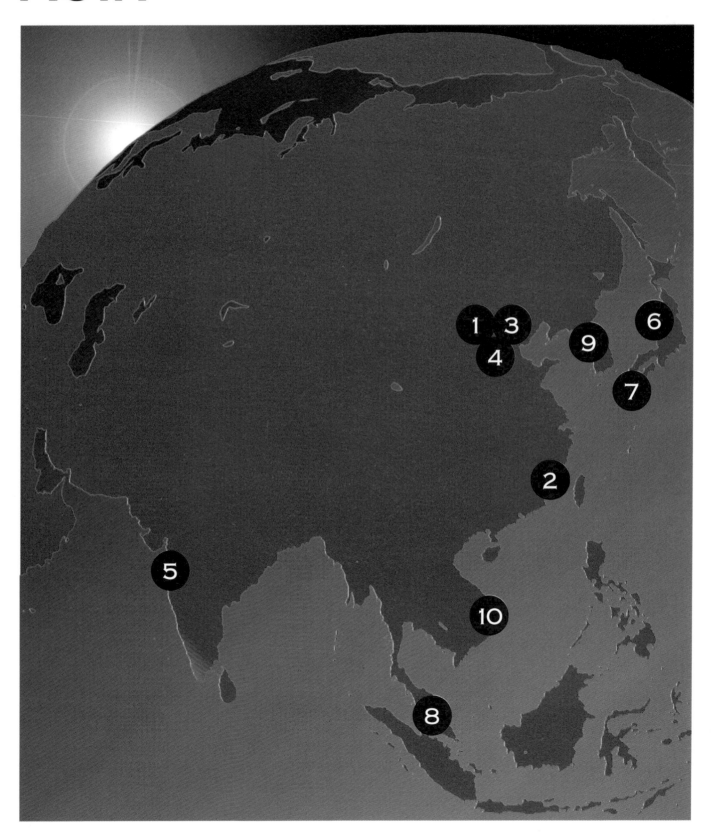

China

Where: Lanxi, Zhejiang
When: 13th October 1970

1 A truck driver Wang Jian Min was told by another driver that a UFO had landed. The driver had stopped his car and refused to go any further. Curious, Wang went to investigate and came across a dome-shaped UFO near the crest of a hill. Beside it were two aliens in silver suits with lamps attached to their helmets. When Wang picked up a crowbar and threatened the beings, they disappeared.

Where: Zhang Po, Fujian
When: 7th July 1977

2 A large audience had gathered to watch the outdoor screening of a Romanian movie. Around 8:30 pm, two massive orange UFOs swept out of the sky, buzzing the assembled moviegoers. The craft came so close that people could feel heat on their heads, sparking a mass panic. In the ensuing chaos, two children were killed.

Where: Beijing
When: 4th December 1995

3 A white egg-shaped object, traveling at 550mph, was sighted by the captain of a airliner.

Where: Beijing
When: 19th December 1996

4 A Boeing 757-200 flying from Beijing to Wuhan collided with a silver UFO, which cracked the outer windshield of the cockpit. The pilot of the plane immediately requested and was granted permission to land at Beijing International Airport, where the incident was briefly reported in the local evening news.

India

Where: Bombay
When: 9th November 1996

5 A miniature UFO, described as being the size of a cricket ball, was witnessed by many people flying through the Kandivli district of Bombay in the early hours of the morning.

Japan

Where: Honshu
When: 17th October 1975

6 Multiple witnesses saw a bright golden disk-shaped UFO over Akita airport, descending to an altitude of about 1500 feet before hovering about 5 miles from the airport. After a few minutes, the craft flew out to sea, where it was tracked by air-traffic control. The UFO was also seen by an airline pilot, Captain Masaru Saito, who described it as resembling two plates put together face to face.

Where: Amakusa Bay
When: 10th December 1996

7 A fisherman found himself stranded at sea after his small motorboat lost power. As he tried to ascertain the cause of the boat's power failure, he found himself bathed in a strange green light, emanating from three UFOs. The trio of objects flew off and immediately afterward, the boat's engine started again.

Malaysia

Where: Central Selangor State
When: September 1995

8 *The New Strait Times* reported that a UFO had been spotted at least four times above forests near the village of Tanjung Sepat Laut.

Crowds gathered at the village and apparently reported seeing a UFO as large as a soccer pitch with two-foot tall occupants, who had long ears and red eyes. Unfortunately there is no photographic evidence of the UFO or its occupants.

South Korea

Where: Seoul
When: 21st November 1996

9 A wave of sightings began over South Korea's capital with an elongated, cylinder-shaped UFO, witnessed by dozens of people in the early hours of the morning. The object, which was captured on video by a Korean television network, hung motionless over the city before moving away and disappearing from view.

Vietnam

Where: Dong Hoi
When: 16th June 1909

10 Three girls saw a glowing object which gave out a low whooshing noise. It flew slowly over the city at approximately 3 am before dropping into the South China Sea, where it was seen by a number of fishermen. The French magazine *L'Astronomie* reported the UFO as a meteor, but it was traveling too slowly to be one.

GLOSSARY

ABDUCTION: The forced abduction of human beings by aliens, frequently, it is claimed, to obtain genetic material or carry out medical tests.

ALIEN: The generic term given to a creature from another world. As well as piloting UFOs, aliens are believed to believed to make regular contact with humans, sometimes in the form of abduction, sometimes in the form of telepathic communion.

ANGEL HAIR: A fine, cobweb-like substance that has appeared on the ground throughout history. While there is no definite scientific explanation for its appearance, some Ufologists claim angel hair is a residue left behind by UFOs, or even still-undiscovered beasts living in the upper reaches of the atmosphere.

ANIMAL MUTILATION: Malicious attacks on animals, usually horses and cattle, that often reveal surgical precision. Some Ufologists claim aliens are responsible, but skeptics blame the attacks on sadistic cranks.

AREA 51: According to many eye-witnesses, the US government has been test-flying aircraft with unusual flying capabilities in the area of Groom Dry Lake in Nevada – otherwise known as Area 51 or Dreamland. Another theory, aired in the movie *Independence Day*, claims that retrieved alien spacecraft and their occupants are held at Area 51.

AURORA, TEXAS: Between November 1896 and May 1897, a series of mysterious objects were seen above the skies of the US. The most famous of these sightings was in the now non-existent town of Aurora, Texas. On 17th April 1897, an airship crashed into a windmill, killing the pilot. When the corpse was discovered, however, it was judged to be "not of this world," and was reportedly buried in the town's cemetery.

AUTOMATON: A creature who walks and behaves like a robot, giving the impression of being remotely controlled.

BACK ENGINEERING: According to Bob Lazar, who claims to be an ex-employee at Area 51, back engineering takes place on alien technology to discover how it works.

BELGIAN TRIANGLE: Between 29th November 1989 and 31st March 1990, there were 11,500 witnesses and 2,500 written reports of a black UFO over the skies of Belgium. The Belgian air force intercepted the object and confirmed it to be a "triangular object" of undetermined origin.

BLACK HELICOPTERS: Usually seen over military establishments, these craft have no markings and are often painted dark colors for camouflage.

BLACK PROJECTS: Unofficial name given to projects involving the manufacture of technologically advanced aircraft.

BLACK TRIANGLE: Many Ufologists believe that the black-triangle UFO is a highly classified spyplane called the Aurora. This craft is capable of traveling at incredible speeds and may contain extraterrestrial technology.

BLUE BOOK: Code name given to a USAF investigation into UFO activity that began in 1952 and closed in 1969.

BONNYBRIDGE: There have been over 2,000 reported sightings of UFOs around this Scottish town since 1992, making it the UK's premier UFO hot spot.

CHANNELING: The process whereby a human agent claims to "channel" the spirit and voice of a long-deceased person or an alien. Alien channelers frequently claim that their extraterrestrial contact has an important message for mankind.

CHUPACABRAS: Also known as the Goatsucker, this creature is thought to have evolved on Puerto Rico, where it is held responsible for a number of savage attacks on humans and animals.

CLOSE ENCOUNTERS: According to the classification system devised by J. Allen Hynek in his book *The UFO Experience*, a CE1 is a visual encounter with a UFO that somehow interacts with the observer or the environment; CE2s refer to physical evidence of a UFO landing; CE3s involve the sighting of aliens as well as UFOs, and CE4s are alien abductions. Ufologists later added the category CE5 to Hynek's system, which refers to regular contact or communion with aliens.

CONTACTEE: Any person who claims to have repeated contact with alien entities. Billy Meier and George Adamski are two of the most famous examples.

CRASH RETRIEVAL: The removal, by the military, of a crashed alien spacecraft – the Roswell incident being a prime example.

CROP CIRCLES: Mysterious formations that appear in fields all over the world, especially Wiltshire in the UK. While many of the culprits responsible for crop circles have revealed their methods, there is still no explanation for some of the most complex shapes, suggesting alien assistance.

CSETI: The Center for the Study of Extraterrestrial Intelligence, which describes itself as "the only worldwide organization dedicated to establishing peaceful and sustainable relations with extraterrestrial life forms." Founded in 1991 by Steven Greer.

CSICOP: The Committee for the Scientific Investigation of Claims of the Paranormal was formed by a group of scientists to investigate unusual phenomena. Taking a skeptical perspective, members have included the late astrophysicist Carl Sagan.

DAYLIGHT DISK: This term is used to cover any sighting of a UFO during daylight hours.

DRAGON PROJECT: Paul Devereux studied the possibility that many UFOs might in fact be natural energy released from the Earth as a result of natural geographical movements. The Dragon Project studies ancient sites and folklore in an effort to see if there is any correlation between UFOs and the importance that our ancestors attributed to certain locations.

DREAMLAND: The popular name for Area 51.

EXTRATERRESTRIAL BIOLOGICAL ENTITY (EBE): The term given to a living, breathing organism, thought to be not human in origin.

EXTRATERRESTRIAL HYPOTHESIS (ETH): The belief that alien beings derive from outer space.

FLAP: The slang term for the controversy following a large number of UFO sightings in an area.

FOO FIGHTER: Strange balls of light that would frequently pace allied fighter planes near the end of World War II. These are now thought to have been Nazi experimental craft, also known as Fueurballs.

GREY: The most commonly reported type of alien, characterized by bulbous heads, almond-shaped eyes and spindly bodies.

GULF BREEZE: An area of Florida where property developer Ed Walters claimed to have filmed some of the most detailed footage of UFOs ever seen. Walters was widely dismissed as a fraud, but the area continues to attract skywatchers.

HANGAR 18: The place within Area 51 were crashed alien spaceships are kept. It has inspired a movie of the same name.

HOLLOW EARTH THEORY: The idea that ancient civilizations, or even alien visitors, thrive in hidden underground places, or in harsh, inaccessible places like the arctic poles.

HUMANOID: An alien being with extremely human-like features.

HYPNOTIC REGRESSION: Technique of hypnosis frequently used to retrieve subconscious memories of alien abduction or similar contact.

IDENTIFIED FLYING OBJECT (IFO): Any anomalous object which turns out to be terrestrially based.

IMPLANTS: Small devices that aliens appear to

have inserted into the nasal cavities, feet and hands of abductees so they could be identified or tracked. Derrel Sims and Dr Roger Leir claim to have surgically removed alien implants.

LENTICULAR CLOUDS: Unusual cloud formations which can look like UFOs. These clouds sometimes form one on top of the other, giving the illusion of a dome-shaped object.

MARFA LIGHTS: Balls of light that appear, change color and dance in the air. Marfa Lights are named after the town of Marfa, Texas, where they have regularly appeared this century. One explanation is UFOs, although there have been no notable reports of aliens landing in the area.

MEN IN BLACK (MIB): Mysterious, otherworldly visitors who are believed to intimidate witnesses of UFO activity into keeping quiet. MIBs, who dress entirely in black, were very prevalent in the 1950s and early 1960s. Also believed to be automatons.

MUFON: Mutual UFO Network, based at Segium, Texas.

NATIONAL SECURITY: The term used by governments to justify investigations into UFOs. Often, however, the authorities use the pretext of national security to conceal information about UFOs from the public.

NOCTURNAL LIGHTS (NL): A visual sighting of an unidentified flying light seen at night. Some 35% to 40% of all UFO reports are said to be NLs.

NORDICS: A breed of alien beings with very human-like characteristics.

OLD NEW MOON PROJECT: Project Old New Moon was the continuation of Project Blue Book to re-investigate the UFO phenomenon. While the USAF denies it exists, Major Donald E. Keyhoe has confirmed the project is real.

OPERATION RIGHT TO KNOW: A body with the aim of obtaining and publishing information about UFOs from the US government.

OUT OF BODY EXPERIENCE (OBE): An experience where a person sees themselves floating above their own body. Skeptics cite OBEs as the explanation for many reported abductions.

RADAR CASES: UFOs detected by radar alone. In recent years, fewer cases involving radar have been reported. This could be the result of a number of factors: perhaps the authorities are getting better at suppressing these reports, or perhaps UFOs themselves have changed, making them harder to detect. Of course, it is also possible that many of the early reports were the result of spurious events and false conclusions, which would be quickly detected by more modern equipment.

RADAR VISUAL: The term given to UFOs observed by the eye and radar. According to J. Allen Hynek's study of UFOs, these make up only about 2% of reports.

REMOTE VIEWING: The ability to "see" a person, house, area or any other given target at distances of up to thousands of miles.

REMOTELY PILOTED VEHICLE (RPV): Any unknown craft which appears to be operated by remote control. The Foo Fighters were often described as being unmanned and operated from the ground.

ROSWELL AUTOPSY: In 1995, a video claiming to include authentic footage of an autopsy on one of the aliens recovered from the Roswell crash, was released by a British businessman. The authenticity of the footage is fiercely debated: skeptics claim the alien corpse was a dummy created by a special effects expert, and point out some suspicious anachronisms, such as curly phone leads.

ROSWELL INCIDENT: Arguably the most famous UFO crash in the world. An alien spaceship allegedly crashed near the Army Air Force Base at Roswell Field, New Mexico, on 2nd July 1947. *The Roswell Daily Record* of 8th July announced that a flying disk had been found. Later that same day, however, the military authorities held a press conference and insisted that the Roswell UFO was in fact the wreckage of a weather balloon. Followers of the flying saucer theory, however, believe that the craft's extraterrestrial occupants were taken away from the wreckage by the authorities.

SCREEN MEMORY: The concept that aliens are able to plant false, or "screen" memories, into the human mind in order to cover up an abduction or other kinds of contact.

TEMPORAL LOBE EPILEPSY: A medical condition whose symptoms are reminiscent of the most commonly reported abduction experiences, namely bright lights, a floating sensation and memory loss.

TWINKLE PROJECT: During the 1940s, reports of a green fireball that kept appearing over New Mexico and the southern states of the US prompted further investigation by the government and the creation of Project Twinkle. A barrage of high-tech (for the time) equipment was set up to record and analyze the anomalous lights to determine whether they really were UFOs or just meteors. Lack of funding and personnel, however, caused the whole project to ground to a halt before any conclusive evidence could be gathered. Green lights are still reported above New Mexico, and observers are adamant they are not meteors.

UFOLOGY: The study of Unidentified Flying Objects. Although not regarded as a science, many adherents, such as implant researcher Derrel Sims, try to apply scientific principles and methods.

UNICAT PROJECT: A project set up by Dr W. Smith and J. Allen Hynek to ascertain whether UFO phenomena were real enough to warrant rigorous scientific investigation. The project, which was remarkably open-minded, came up with some fascinating conclusions. It stated, for example, that there were differences in alien and human interaction and that abductions were always pre-planned rather than accidents – even if the abductee at first thought they had stumbled across the aliens purely by chance.

UNIDENTIFIED FLYING OBJECT (UFO): The general term given to any aircraft of unknown origin. A wide variety of UFOs have been reported, with disk, cigar and triangle shapes being the most common.

URD PROJECT: Like the UNICAT project, URD set out to determine whether UFOs were worthy of funding for further investigation. The URD project decided, after collecting over 150 cases, that UFOs were real enough to warrant a serious investigation. What really convinced the participants that there was cause for further research was the similarity between UFO accounts from unrelated sources.

VENUS: This planet is commonly misidentified as a UFO because of its magnitude and tendency to shimmer in the night sky.

VOKSHOD SPACE MISSIONS: As with the US lunar missions, there is speculation that cosmonauts of the former Soviet Union experienced close encounters with UFOs while in space. In the mid-1960s, the Soviet craft *Vokshod 1* was apparently joined briefly by some fast-moving flying saucers. Mysterious magnetic disturbances also played havoc with instrument panels, and there were rumors that the cosmonauts lost contact with mission control for an unspecified period. The former Soviet Union never confirmed the stories, however.

WAVERIDER: An experimental joint USAF/NASA aircraft, able to fly unpiloted.

WISE BABY DREAMS: An expression related to the theory that aliens plan to create a hybrid species from a human and an extraterrestrial. Several female abductees have reported dreams where they see a baby that would seem to fit this hybrid description, as well as displaying signs of exceptional intelligence. Some pregnant abductees claim under hypnotic regression that their fetuses have been removed, and other women have reportedly been allowed to see the hybrid child they helped produce.

XENOMORPH: A less commonly used technical term for any alien entity.

ZETA RETICULI: Following Betty and Barney Hill's revelation of an alien abduction in 1961, they also produced a sketch of a "star chart" that the pair had been shown by their abductors. These sketches were examined by Marjorie Fish, an expert on constellations, who deduced that the aliens must have come from the planets around the stars Zeta Reticuli 1 and 2. Most astronomers are skeptical.

UFO Contact Groups

Have you seen an Unidentified Flying Object or suspect you may have been abducted? Do you want to join a UFO group but don't know of one in your area? The following is a list of UFO-related organizations worldwide, intended to help people find the most suitable contact or support group for them.

United States

Abductees Anonymous
266 W. El Paso Avenue, Clovis, CA 93611-7119

APRO
(Aerial Phenomena Research Organization)
3910 East Kleindale, Tucson, AZ 85712

CAUS
(Citizens Against UFO Secrecy)
PO Box 218, Coventry, CT 06238

CSETI
(The Center for the Study of Extraterrestrial Intelligence)
PO Box 15401, Asheville, NC 28813

CSICOP
(Committee for the Scientific Investigation of Claims of the Paranormal)
PO Box 703, Amherst, NY 14266
email info@csicop.org

CUFOS
(J. Allen Hynek Center for UFO Studies)
2457 W. Peterson Avenue, Chicago, ILL 60659
Tel: (773) 271 3611
Fax: (773) 465 1898

The Fleetwood Project
PO Box 1356, San Bruno, CA 94066

International UFO Museum & Research Center
400 North Main, Roswell, NM 88202

Intruders Foundation
PO Box 30233, New York, NY 10011
Tel/Fax: (212) 645 5278

ISCNI
(Institute for the Study of Contact with Non-human Intelligence)
3463 State Street #440, Santa Barbara, CA 93105
Tel: (800) 563 8500
Fax: (805) 563 8503

LIUFON
(Long Island UFO Network)
PO Box 1692, Riverhead, NY 11901

Massachusetts Center for the Study of Aerial Phenomena
43 Harrison Street, Reading, MA 01867

MUFON
(Mutual UFO Network)
103 Oldtowne Road, Seguin, TX 78155-4099
Tel: (512) 379 9216

New York Fortean Society
Box 20024, New York, NY 10025

NSRC
(National Sighting Research Center)
PO Box 76, Emerson, NJ 07630

Operation Right To Know
PO Box 2911, Hyatsville, MD 20784

OPUS
(Organization for Paranormal Understanding and Support)
PO Box 273273, Concord, CA 94527
Tel/Fax: (510) 689 2666

PUFOG
(Portland UFO Group)
PO Box 998, Wilsonville, OR 97070
Tel: (503) 538 0836

San Diego UFO Society
PO Box 34351, San Diego, CA 92103
Tel: (619) 299 9157

Stargate International
PO Box 85159, Tucson, Arizona, AZ 85754-5159
Tel: (520) 882 9544

TASK
(Tri-State Advocates for Scientific Knowledge)
2477 Hudson Avenue, Cincinnati, OH 45212
Tel/Fax: (513) 351 4951
Email: task@fuse.net
http://users1.ee.net/pmason/TASK.html

UFOIRC
(UFO Information Retrieval Center)
3131 W. Cochise Drive #158, Phoenix, AZ 85051-9501
Tel: (602) 997 1523

Canada

AUFORA
(Alberta UFO Research Association)
162 Pumpridge Place S.W., Calgary, Alberta T2V 5E6
http://www.aufora.org

The Mutual UFO Network of Ontario
3058 Fifth Line West #7, Mississauga, Ontario L5L 5WA

SOS OVNI Quebec
Box 143, St. Jean-sur-Richelieu, Quebec J3B 6Z1
ocipe@chucara.hexacom.com

UFORIC
(UFO Research Institute of Canada)
Dept 25, 1665 Robson Street, Vancouver, British Columbia V6G 3C2

United Kingdom

BEAMS HQ
(British Earth and Aerial Mystery Society)
7 North Drive, Shortstown, Bedford, Bedfordshire MK42 0TL
Tel: (01234) 403461

BUFORA
(British UFO Research Association)
BM BUFORA, London WC1N 3XX
Tel: (01352) 732473

BUFOS
(Bolton UFO Society)
134 Chorley New Road, Horwich,
Bolton BL6 5QN
Tel: (01204) 695719

CONTACT INTERNATIONAL
11 Ousley Close, New Marston,
Oxford OX3 0JS

CUFORG
(Cornwall UFO Research Group)
24 Carrine Road, Truro,
Cornwall TR1 3XB
Tel: (01872) 76381

EMUFORA
(East Midlands UFO Research
Association)
8 Roosa Close, Hempshill Vale,
Bulwell, Nottingham NG6 7BL

ENIGMA
16 Clare Close, Off Thomas More Way,
East Finchley, London N2 0UY
Tel: (0181) 343 3910

GLOBAL UFO INVESTIGATION SYSTEMS
Unit 4C, The Modern Moulds Business
Centre, Harewood Road, Littlehampton,
West Sussex BN17 7AU
Tel: (01903) 520025 or
(0161) 945 0257
Fax: (01903) 721144

LAPIS
(Lancaster Aerial Phenomena
Investigation Society)
239 Devonshire Road, Blackpool,
Lancashire FY2 0TW
Tel: (01253) 356821

MAPIT
(Manchester Anomalous Phenomena
Investigation Team)
3 Paighton Drive, Ashton-On-Mersey,
Sale, Cheshire M33 5H
Tel: (0161) 905 3047

NORTHANTS UFO FORUM
108 Malcolm Drive,
Northampton NN5 5NH
Tel: (01604) 756153

OPERATION RIGHT TO KNOW
20 Newton Gardens, Ripon,
North Yorkshire HG4 1QF
Tel: (01765) 602898

PLYMOUTH UFO RESEARCH GROUP
40 Albert Road, Stoke, Plymouth,
Devon PL2 1AE
Tel: (01752) 562255

PMS
(Paranormal Management Systems)
PO Box 2749, Brighton BN2 2DR
Tel: (01273) 690424
Email: pms@interquest.compulink.co.uk

ROCHDALE UFO RESEARCH GROUP
116 Louise Street, Smallbridge,
Rochdale, Lancashire

SCOTTISH EARTH MYSTERIES RESEARCH
PO Box 16370, Glasgow, Scotland G20 8PX

SCOTTISH UNEXPLAINED PHENOMENA RESEARCH
49 Limefield Crescent, Bathgate,
Scotland EH48 1RF
Tel: (01506) 635184

SKYSEARCH
PO Box 2507, Saltdean, Brighton BN2 8NE
Tel: (01273) 300805

SOUTHAMPTON UFO GROUP
25 Weston Grove Road, Woolston,
Southampton, Hants SO2 9EF
Tel: (01703) 448194

SPUR
(Society for Paranormal & UFO Research)
26 Cardigan Close, Batley,
West Yorkshire WF17 6PR
Tel: (01421) 010710

STAFFORDSHIRE UFO GROUP
11 Sandy Lane, Rugeley,
Staffordshire WS15 2LB
Tel: (01889) 576771

STRANGE PHENOMENA INVESTIGATIONS
29 Kent Road, Alloa,
Clackmannanshire, Scotland FK10 2JN
Tel: (01259) 210714

STRANGE PHENOMENA STUDIES
PO Box 2677, Poole, Dorset BH15 1XE

TRIBAL COMMUNION UFO RESEARCH GROUP
75 Clactron Road, Paulsgrove,
Portsmouth, Hants PO6 3QS
Tel: (01705) 619772

TRUTHSEEKERS INTERNATIONAL
25 Upper Canning Street, Ton'Pentre,
Mid Glamorgan CF1 7HG
Tel: (01443) 437853

UFOLOGY & SUPERNATURAL STUDIES
8 Trafford House, Minutern Street,
London N1 6TJ
Tel: (0171) 684 0775

UK UFO NETWORK
6 Aspbury Croft, Castle Bromwich,
Birmingham B36 9TD

WALES FEDERATION OF INDEPENDENT UFOLOGISTS
PO Box 43, Rhyl, Flintshire,
Wales LL18 1YW
Tel: (01745) 860573

YUFORIA
19 Glenfall Yate, Bristol BS17 4LX
Tel: (01454) 312513

AUSTRALASIA
AUSTRALIAN UFO ABDUCTION STUDY CENTRE
GPO 1894, Adelaide, South Australia 5001

INDEPENDENT UFO RESEARCH
PO Box 783, Kogarah, NSW 2217

MELBOURNE NEXUS ASSOCIATION
PO Box 235, Kangaroo Ground,
Victoria 3097

MUFON
PO Box 27117, Mt Roskill, Auckland 1030,
New Zealand

MUFON AUSTRALIA/ CONTINENTAL
GPO 1894, Adelaide, South Australia 5001

TUFOIC
(Tasmanian UFO Investigation Centre)
PO Box 174, South Hobart, Tasmania 7004

INDEX

PICTURE CREDITS

Page 10:   Top Left: Fortean Picture Library
Top Right - Bob Schott
Bottom Left - Derrel Sims
Bottom Right - Fortean Picture
Library

Page 11:   Top Left - Fortean Picture Library
Top RIght - Steve Alexander
Bottom Left and Right - Paragon
Publishing

Page 12:   Intro Pic - Paragon Publishing
Top Left - Paragon Publishing
Middle - Russian UFO Society
Middle - Fortean Picture Library
Bottom - Fortean Picture Library

Page 14:   Top Left - Paragon Publishing
Bottom Left - Paragon Publishing
Bottom Right - Russian UFO Society
Bottom Right - Russian UFO Society

Page 15:   Top Left - Russian UFO Society
Top Right - Russian UFO Society
Bottom - Russian UFO Society

Page 16:   Top Left - Paragon Publishing
Top Right - Russian UFO Society
Bottom Right - Fortean Picture
Library

Page 17:   Top Left - Paragon Publishing
Top Right - Fortean Picture Library

Page 18:   Top - Paragon Publishing
Bottom - Fortean Picture Library

Page 19:   Bottom - Fortean Picture Library

Page 22:   Top - Glen Campbell
Middle - Paragon Publishing

Page 23:   Top - Glen Campbell
Middle - Paragon Publishing
Bottom - Paragon Publishing

Page 24:   Top Left - Russian UFO Society
Top Right - Russian UFO Society
Middle - Glen Campbell
Middle - Paragon Publishing

Page 25:   Top - Russian UFO Society
Middle - Russian UFO Society
Bottom Left - Fortean Picture Library
Bottom Left - Fortean Picture Library

Page 26:   Middle - Fortean Picture Library
Bottom - Fortean Picture Library

Page 27:   Top - Paragon Publishing
Bottom Left - Paragon Publishing
Bottom Right - Paragon Publishing

Page 28:   Top Left - Fortean Picture Library
Middle - Genesis iii Publishing
Middle - Fortean Picture Library
Bottom - Carlos Diaz
Intro - Ed Walters

Page 30:   Middle Left - Fortean Picture Library
Middle Right - Paragon Publishing
Bottom - Paragon Publishing

Page 31:   Top Left - Paragon Publishing
Top Right - Paragon Publishing
Bottom - Paragon Publishing

Page 32:   Top - Paragon Publishing
Middle - Paragon Publishing

Page 33:   Middle Left - Fortean Picture Library
Middle Right - Paragon Publishing
Bottom - Fortean Picture Library

Page 34:   Bottom Left - Ed Walters
Bottom Right - Ed Walters

Page 35:   Top Right - Paragon Publishing
Middle - BEAMS
Bottom - Empire Entertainment

Page 36:   Top - Carlos Diaz
Bottom - Fortean Picture Library
Bottom Right - Fortean Picture
Library

Page 37:   Top - Genesis iii Publishing
Middle - Carlos Diaz
Bottom - Genesis iii Publishing

Page 38:   Paragon Publishing

Page 39:   Top - Paragon Publishing
Middle - Paragon Publishing
Bottom - Paragon Publishing

Page 40:   Top Left - Fortean Picture Library
Top Right - Fortean Picture Library
Bottom - Fortean Picture Library

Page 41:   Top Right - Alan F Alford
Middle - Fortean Picture Library
Bottom - Ray Santilli

Page 42:   Middle - NASA
Bottom - NASA/ Bob Dean

Page 43:   Top - NASA / Bob Dean
Middle - NASA
Bottom - NASA

Page 44:   Left - NASA
Right - NASA

Page 45:   Top - Bob Dean / NASA
Middle - NASA
Bottom - NASA

Page 46:   Left - Paragon Publishing
Right - Bob Dean

Page 47:   Top Left - Sunday Times
Top Right - Lockheed Martin
Middle - Bob Dean / NASA
Bottom - Bob Dean / NASA

Page 48:   Top Left - Fortean Picture Library
Middle - Fortean Picture Library
Middle - Fortean Picture Library
Bottom - Robert Morning Sky
Intro - Fortean Picture Library

Page 50:   Top - Fortean Picture Library
Bottom - Chris Kenworthy

Page 51:   Top - Chris Kenworthy
Bottom - Chris Kenworthy

Page 52:   Top - Bob Schott
Bottom - Fortean Picture Library

Page 53:   Top - Bob Schott
Bottom - Fortean Picture Library

Page 54:   Left - Paragon Publishing
Bottom Right - Fortean Picture
Library

Page 56:   Bottom - Paragon Publishing

Page 57:   Bottom - Paragon Publishing

Page 58:   Top - Fortean Picture Library

Page 59:   Top Left - Fortean Picture Library
Top Right - Paragon Publishing
Middle - Fortean Picture Library

Page 60:   Top Left - Fortean Picture Library
Top Right - Paragon Publishing
Middle - Fortean Picture Library
Bottom - Fortean Picture Library

Page 61:   Top - Thomas Feiner
Bottom - Ray Santilli

Page 62:   Top - Fortean Picture Library
Middle - Ray Santilli
Bottom - Paragon Publishing

Page 63:   Top Left - Ray Santilli
Middle - Robert Morning Sky
Bottom - Fortean Picture Library

Page 64:   Bottom - Paragon Publishing

Page 65:   Bottom - Paragon Publishing

Page 66:   Middle - Fortean Picture Library
Bottom - Fortean Picture Library

Page 67:   Top - Fortean Picture Library
Middle - Paragon Publishing
Bottom - Fortean Picture Library

Page 68:   Top Left - Pauline Delcour-Minn
Middle - Fortean Picture library
Middle - Fortean Picture Library
Bottom - Fortean Picture Library
Intro - Fortean Picture Library

Page 70:   Top - Fortean Picture Library
Bottom - Fortean Picture Library

Page 71:   Top Left - Fortean Picture Library
Top Right - Fortean Picture Library
Middle - Fortean Picture Library
Bottom - Fortean Picture Library

Page 72:   Top - Fortean Picture Library
Bottom - Fortean Picture Library

Page 73:   Top Left - Paragon Publishing
Top Right - Paragon Publishing
Bottom - Fortean Picture Library

Page 74:   Top Left - Fortean Picture Library

Page 75:   Top Left - Empire Entertainment
Top Right - Fortean Picture Library

Page 76:   Left - Peter Hough

Page 77:   Bottom - Paragon Publishing

Page 78:   Left - Paragon Publishing

Page 79:   Middle - Paragon Publishing
Bottom - Fortean Picture Library

Page 80:   Top Left - Fortean Picture Library
Top Right - Pauline Delcour-Minn
Bottom - Fortean Picture Library

Page 81:   Top - Fortean Picture Library
Bottom - Pauline Delcour-Minn

Page 82:   Top - Fortean Picture Library
Bottom - Fortean Picture Library

Page 83:   Top - Fortean Picture Library
Middle - Fortean Picture Library
Bottom - Fortean Picture Library

Page 84:   Middle - Derrel Sims
Bottom - Derrel Sims/
Dr Roger Leir

Page 85:   Top Left - Derrel Sims/
Dr Roger Leir
Top Right - Pauline Delcour-Minn

Page 86:   Top Left - Alan F Alford
Middle - Steve Alexander
Middle - Fortean Picture Library
Bottom - Paragon Publishing
Intro - Genesis iii Publishing

Page 88:   Top Left - Fortean Picture Library
Top Right - Fortean Picture Library
Bottom - Erich Von Daniken

Page 89:   Middle Left - Maria Reiche
Middle Right - Alan F Alford
Bottom - Alan F Alford

Page 90:   Top Left - Alan F Alford
Top Right - Alan F Alford
Bottom - Paragon Publishing

Page 91:   Top - Alan F Alford
Middle Left - Alan F Alford
Middle Right - Fortean Picture
Library
Bottom - Paragon Publishing

Page 92:   Top - Fortean Picture Library
Bottom - Fortean Picture Library

Page 93:   Top - Fortean Picture Library
Middle Left - Fortean Picture Library
Middle Right - Fortean Picture
Library
Bottom - Fortean Picture Library

Page 94:   Top - Paragon Publishing
Left - Paragon Publishing
Bottom - Paragon Publishing

Page 95:   Top - Fortean Picture Library
Middle - Fortean Picture Library
Bottom - Paragon Publishing

Page 96:   Top - Genesis iii Publishing
Middle - Fortean Picture Library
Bottom - Genesis iii Publishing

Page 97:   Top - Genesis iii Publishing
Middle - Genesis iii Publishing

Page 98:   Top - CSETI
Middle - Fortean Picture library
Bottom - Fortean Picture Library

Page 99:   Top - Fortean Picture Library
Middle - Fortean Picture Library
Bottom - Paragon Publishing

Page 100: Top - Fortean Picture Library
Middle - Paragon Publishing
Bottom - Tim Rifat

Page 101: Right - Paragon Publishing

Page 102: Top Left - Steve Alexander
Top Right - Steve Alexander
Bottom - Paragon Publishing

Page 103: Top Left - Steve Alexander
Top Right - Steve Alexander
Middle - Steve Alexander
Bottom - Paragon Publishing

Page 104: Top Left - Steve Alexander
Top Right - Steve Alexander
Middle - Steve Alexander
Bottom - Steve Alexander

Page 105: Top - Steve Alexander
Middle - Steve Alexander
Right - Steve Alexander
Bottom - Steve Alexander.